HANDEL AND HIS ORBIT

Da Capo Press Music Reprint Series

MUSIC EDITOR
BEA FRIEDLAND
Ph.D., City University of New York

HANDEL AND HIS ORBIT

BY

P. ROBINSON, B.A. (Oxon.)

NEW FOREWORD BY
JENS PETER LARSEN

DA CAPO PRESS · NEW YORK · 1979

Library of Congress Cataloging in Publication Data

Robinson, Percy, 1863-
  Handel and his orbit.

  (Da Capo Press music reprint series)
  Reprint of the 1908 ed. published by
Sherratt & Hughes, London.
  Includes index.
  1. Händel, Georg Friedrich, 1685-1759.
I. Title.
ML410.H13R5 1979   780'.92'4   79-13828
ISBN 0-306-79522-1

This Da Capo Press edition of *Handel and His Orbit*
is an unabridged republication of the edition
published in London in 1908 by Sherratt & Hughes,
supplemented with a new foreword by Jens Peter Larsen.

New Foreword copyright 1979 by Jens Peter Larsen.

Published by Da Capo Press, Inc.
A Subsidiary of Plenum Publishing Corporation
227 West 17th Street, New York, N.Y. 10011

FOREWORD

REFLECTIONS ON HANDEL'S "BORROWING" PRACTICES

Was Handel a plagiarist? Did he consciously rob other composers of their music, using themes and ideas — even whole movements — composed by others, as models or as parts of his own compositions without proper acknowledgment? This question was intimated more than a hundred years ago, and about 1890 a series of works was edited by Chrysander, the great German Handel scholar, called *Sources for Handel's Works* ("Quellen zu Händels Werken"). But it was above all the works by Sedley Taylor *(The Indebtedness of Handel to Works by Other Composers,* 1906) and Percy Robinson *(Handel and His Orbit,* 1908) which focused on Handel's "borrowings" with such emphasis that the problem called forth almost a whole literature of its own. In his bibliography of Handel writings K. Sasse lists some seventy books and articles discussing this delicate subject.

The question of Handel's "borrowings" might perhaps seem rather simple, considering the comprehensive material available, but is more complicated than it may appear. That Handel *did* use a great amount of "borrowed" material in his works is plain. But why did he? How did he use the material? Was this something otherwise unheard of, or did other composers act in a similar way? And was it mainly a question of creative procedure or of morals? If a question of morals, why were no objections voiced in Handel's lifetime? Are we altogether able today to make an unprejudiced evaluation of this problem as the contemporaries of Handel would have seen it?

These are some of the questions to be pondered if we want to understand the nature and meaning of the "borrowings." But before we try to discuss the "moral" problem, we must regard the problem of "borrowing" in a broader sense: the use of existing musical themes or constructions, changed or virtually unchanged, as the basis for new compositions — not just taken over from the works of others, but to a large extent also from the composer's own earlier works. In other words, we must try to approach the specific *creative* procedure connected with the "borrowings," before we venture an evaluation of the moral problems involved.

In the sixteenth century it was quite a normal procedure to adapt the music of a motet or a chanson for a mass; it might be music by another composer or it might be by the composer himself, as when Palestrina used his own motet *Tu Es Petrus* as the basis for a mass. The reason for this adaptation would scarcely be lack of invention on the part of the composer; he might easily have composed the mass without using "borrowed" material. Two other motives for making use of the motet as a model may be suggested here: a composer might be fond of the music of his motet and wishes to give it a chance of being heard more often; he might find in the music unspent reserves calling for his creative power, and judges it a more interesting and rewarding project to unfold its hidden possibilities than to start an altogether new composition.

This procedure of transforming a composition — or part of it — into a new one (the so-called parody principle) was apparently less common in the seventeenth century, but it is a very characteristic feature in the music of Bach and Handel. Bach excelled in adjusting secular cantatas to new texts to serve as church cantatas *(Christmas Oratorio),* and he arranged part of the *St. Matthew Passion* from a funeral cantata for Prince Leopold of Anhalt-Köthen, so that the fine music would not remain buried with the prince. He would also find early concertos for violin or for violin and oboe and arrange them for one or two harpsichords, when such pieces were needed in his later years in Leipzig.

There are quite similar types of arrangements in Handel's works, vocal as well as instrumental. And there is the same ambition to save fine occasional compositions from oblivion by adjusting them to new texts and functions: the famous Coronation Anthems (1727) were used to adorn oratorios, and so was the Funeral Anthem (1737), which (with slight alterations of the text) was made to serve as the first part of *Israel in Egypt.*

However, the most interesting type of "borrowings," of adjusting pre-existent music to serve in a new context, is not the direct transference of larger units, but the reshaping of a single movement or the completely new and surprising development of one short memorable phrase. This special procedure is a characteristic Handel feature, to such a degree that it seems impossible to name any other composer as a counterpart to him in this respect. A most typical example of the reshaping of single movements is a group of four choruses in the *Messiah,* among them "For unto us a child is born"; they were all originally secular chamber duets, but have been transformed to choral settings much superior to their models. Handel's music is full of such brilliant transformations, changing phrases and passages which might appear to have found their final shape into a new, definitive mold — remarkable not for its complexity, but rather for its natural simplicity and clarity.

It is an established fact that Bach and Handel were both fond of re-using pre-existent music of their own, in Bach's case perhaps mostly to save it from being put aside, in Handel's obviously also from a strong interest in reshaping as a creative procedure in itself. Yet another observable difference was their treatment of music taken from other composers. The one really outstanding case of Bach's "borrowings," cited again and again, is his arrangement of concertos by Vivaldi and others as concertos for harpsichord or organ without any indication of the composers' names. Not until about a hundred years ago were they recognized as arrangements, not authentic Bach concertos. However, Bach has never been seriously accused of plagiarism on account of these works.

Handel "borrowed" much more frequently than Bach, and from a wider range of composers. Once again, Handel's artistry in this practice must be considered: even if he reshapes a complete work, the most surprising examples of "borrowings" are found in single parts and movements, or just themes and passing phrases. The best survey of this is undoubtedly given in Sedley Taylor's book (1906). Of course the volumes of *Sources for Handel's Works* edited by Chrysander are very valuable too, but they concentrate on a limited number of works and merely allude to the relevant Handel parallels without quoting the examples directly. In Taylor's book, works by nine (?) different composers are quoted, forty-nine examples in all (though only a selection), and in each instance the musical example carefully places the Handel quotation against the quotation of the corresponding "borrowed" material. Nobody can deny that Taylor was justified in using as a subtitle for his book: *A Presentation of Evidence*.

However, Taylor's book is not a pure and simple documentation, only for the sake of evidence. He had an idea, a message to convey: there was something rotten in the morals of Handel. This is made quite clear in his final summing up (p. 187):

> That the musical world is the richer for the way in which Handel used thematic materials due to his predecessors and his contemporaries can hardly be doubted. Surely, however, he could equally well have conferred that boon if he had openly acknowledged his obligations to other composers. But, as matters stand, the fact remains that he accepted, indeed practically claimed, merit for what he must have known was not his own work. That this was wrong can, it appears to me, be denied by those only who are prepared to estimate the morality of an act according to the amount of genius shown in performing it.

Here speaks a good Victorian. His verdict is not based on a general understanding of the difference between eighteenth- and twentieth-century tra-

ditions in matters of this kind. The Buononcini affair from 1731 is reported
rather extensively, and the following conclusion is presented (p. 176):

> This correspondence shows conclusively that plagiarism was regarded by
> educated musicians in the eighteenth century as it is regarded by them in
> the twentieth. A charge of being a "Plagiary" is what no man who has
> "regard for his own fame and reputation" can afford to leave unrebutted.

Taylor's interpretation of the problem was certainly in agreement with the
moral principles of his time. But there were other interpretations very far from
his. Taylor quotes (p. 186) some interesting considerations by A.J. Balfour:

> If the main objection to robbery consists in the fact that the victim of the
> robbery is injured by it, Handel's appropriation of the music of his pre-
> decessors would seem to be innocent, if not meritorious. So far from their
> being injured by it in the quarter in which injury was alone possible,
> namely, their reputation, it is not too much to say that their whole reputation
> is entirely founded on it. Who would take the slightest interest in Urio if
> Handel had not condescended to use his "Te Deum" in "Saul" and the
> "Dettingen"? Who would ever have heard of Erba if Handel had not im-
> mortalised him by introducing parts of his "Magnificat" into "Israel"? The
> fact is that Handel has not cheated them *out of* their due meed of fame, he
> has cheated them *into* it.

The main opponent to Taylor's verdict was, however, Percy Robinson, who,
after a couple of preliminary articles in *Musical Times* and *Sammelbände der
internationalen Musikgesellschaft,* published his book *Handel and His Orbit* in
1908. Unlike Sedley Taylor's, this is not a book of documentation, but of
argumentation. But like Taylor, Robinson also had a strong conviction about the
question of Handel's "borrowings": he did as much urge a "non-guilty" verdict
as Taylor a finding of "guilty." Robinson's discussion of the matter is determined
mainly by three aspects: a demonstration of prejudice in the traditional approach
to Handel's music; a commendable striving towards an understanding of the
problem in the light of eighteenth-, not twentieth-century views; and a specific
interpretation of three central sources of Handel's "borrowings" as works by
Handel himself, not by the alleged Italian composers Erba, Urio, and Stradella.

Robinson's stressing of prejudice in the approach to Handel is perhaps of
less interest today, but it was certainly founded on facts. A strong reaction to
Handel's long reign as the accepted "great master of English music" had caused
a notable hostility, encountered frequently in contemporary writings. He was
accused of having "exercised a repressing effect on English music" for generations; the interest in his "borrowings" may well be seen, to some extent, as part
of the attempt to overturn his statue. But aside from this quite special type of
prejudice, the understanding of baroque music — and, not least, of baroque

opera — could scarcely have been more prejudiced than in a time still over-whelmingly stamped by the ideas and music of Richard Wagner.

The central — and the best part — of Robinson's book is his discussion of eighteenth-century traditions and views on the problems of "borrowings." Unlike Taylor, he does not consider the problem from the point of view of morality — still less, Victorian morality — but he tries to build up a background of eighteenth-century views and habits. He stresses the fact that Handel's "borrow-ings" were not unknown to his contemporaries; part were carried out quite openly, when Handel "borrowed" from printed, recently published works by others.[1] Nevertheless there were no reactions to them, not even from his compet-itors and enemies. It fell to the age of Victorianism to raise the problem se-riously, ignoring changed traditions in the creative arts.

The last part of the book is devoted to Robinson's favorite idea about Handel's authorship of three works, otherwise claimed to be by Erba, Urio, and Stradella. The known sources for the *Magnificat* by Erba (?) and the *Te Deum* by Urio (?) seem to be of English origin, and this, as well as Handel's rather palpable "borrowings" from these two works, might find a natural explanation in the acceptance of Handel's authorship. But, in spite of Robinson's elaborate defense of this hypothesis it seems difficult to accept — founded on wishful thinking rather than on facts. Though Handel used motives and phrases, and occasionally almost whole movements from these works, the general impression of them — and especially of those parts Handel was not interested in using — cannot confirm the assumption of his authorship. In the spring and summer of 1707 Handel composed two similar works which give a true impression of his style and his early developed mastery in this field: the psalms *Dixit Dominus* and *Laudate Pueri* (second version). Compared to these authentic compositions, the two questionable works cannot — in spite of Handel's many quotations from them — seriously be accepted as authentic Handel works. They are stylistically unconvincing, and they are without the touch of genius, the unifying power, melting the parts together.

---

[1]Robinson's view is strongly confirmed in a couple of letters from Jennens, author of several librettos to Handel's oratorios, written to a friend at the beginning of 1743. They were unknown until recently, when they were offered for sale at Christie's in London (on July 4, 1973). In the first letter (January 17, 1743) he writes:

> ... I told you before that one of the Composers in my Box was good, I mean Scarlatti: & I shall not condemn the rest without a fair Trial. Handel has borrow'd a dozen of the Pieces & I dare say I shall catch him stealing from them; as I have formerly, both from Scarlatti & Vinci. ...

In a second letter (February 21, 1743) he returns to the question of Handel's "borrowings" in the following words:

> ... I am sorry I mention'd my Italian Musick to Handel, for I don't like to have him borrow from them who has so much a better fund of his own. ...

The question of Handel's "borrowings" has been taken up in many books and articles following Taylor and Robinson, with changing evaluations of the crucial problem and additional lists of examples. One special question has been given particular attention: why was Handel's use of "borrowings" more extensive at some periods than at others, and in particular, why was it exceptionally characteristic in works written about 1737–1738 *(Israel in Egypt)*? As early as in the Oxford History of Music (Vol. IV, 1902) Fuller-Maitland touched upon that question:

> One other plea that has never, so far as we know, been set up in his defence, is that it is at least possible that his illness of 1737, while it had not permanently affected his mental well-being in the least, may have caused him to forget the source of some of the Mss. in his possession, and he may have mistaken the unnamed copy of Erba's Magnificat for a work of his own, when he wanted materials for *Israel*.

However, it. was mainly a passage in Dent's *Handel* (1934) which called attention to the question about the concentration of "borrowings" in *Israel in Egypt* (pp. 105–108).

> A careful study of these alterations suggests a reason for Handel's action which seems not to have occurred to any previous writer on the subject. No one seems to have noted hitherto that Handel's borrowings begin in 1736 on a small scale, and become more frequent in 1737, after which they develop into a regular habit. It seems only natural therefore to connect them with Handel's mental collapse; it became acute in the spring of 1737, but it may well have been approaching in the previous year.
>
> There is no need to go so far as to suggest that Handel suffered from moral insanity and was incapable of distinguishing between right and wrong. . . . But after his attack of paralysis there may well have been occasional moments when Handel could not make up his mind to write down an idea of his own, but may very likely have found that once he had an idea ready on paper before him, whether that of another composer or an old one of his own, he could then continue to compose, and often make alterations in the music under his eyes which transformed it from a commonplace into a masterpiece.[2]

---

[2]I cannot resist the temptation to include here some comments on the question made by Dent in a letter to me shortly after the publication of his book. During a visit to Copenhagen in 1935 he had given me a copy, and when, after reading it, I thanked him in a note, naturally I commented on his interesting hypothesis on the "borrowings." From his answer to my remarks I quote the following passage:

> My hypothesis concerning the borrowings came to me all at once when I was writing the book. Certainly I knew Sedley Taylor very well and I helped him with his book, but at that time we did not think about an exact timetable for the borrowings, and it was only when I went over the biographical material thoroughly for my own book that I first understood how

The validity of Dent's hypothesis may perhaps be questioned. Percy Young raised a noteworthy objection to it in his *Handel* (1947, p. 234):

> To revert to the more orthodox doctrine of borrowing, we find Professor Edward J. Dent suggesting that, as Handel used other people's music more intensively after 1737, he needed thematic stimulus of this order on account of the paralysis which had affected the state of his mind. This led speculation up an unpleasant avenue. That form of paralysis which has the direst effect on the mind is syphilitic paralysis. This would have blunted Handel's moral sense and accounted for large-scale depredation of other men's thoughts to an unprecedented degree. Moreover, Handel went to recuperate at Aix-la-Chapelle, which was the European centre for the treatment (such as it was in those days) of venereal disease. Fortunately for Handel's reputation, he did not decline into general paralysis of the insane, which would certainly have been the case had he contracted the French pox. He suffered on two occasions a severe cerebral thrombosis, and recovered in quick time because of efficient vascularity. Such recovery would have left his mentality unimpaired. His "maggots" and his moroseness should therefore not be exaggerated. Since it is the fashion of the day to associate genius with either homosexuality or venereal disease, it had better be stated that there is no particle of evidence to suggest that Handel was tainted by either.

I am not able to evaluate the medical aspects of Handel's illness, but I clearly remember discussing it with the late fine Handel scholar and doctor, James Hall, who expressed very much the same view as Percy Young.

The focusing on the period 1737–1738 has until now been directed only towards the question of a possible connection between Handel's increased use of "borrowings" and his illness, the character of which may still seem somewhat obscure. But there is another important turn in Handel's professional life just at the same time which may have some bearing on his choice of "prefabricated" material. In June 1738 his long-time singer Strada left London, and in July, Heidegger, the opera manager, announced that Handel had given up his dealings with the singers and that he would "give up the Undertaking for next Year." Handel, who had not composed any oratorio the preceding five years, set out at once to compose *Saul,* and later, in the fall, *Israel in Egypt,* counting on a new performance style and, more or less, a changed musical style. And here the

---

serious Handel's mental illness had been. The well-meaning biographers have taken care to mitigate this episode. Taylor's book in fact is very instructive; and I, who knew him so well, always remember the tiny old man who practically turned himself into a martyr, so far as normal life was concerned, in his fanatical regard for absolute truth and justice. He was extraordinarily kind and filled with love for his fellow-men; but he was dangerous in that he always spoke the bare truth without regard to the consequences. Thus the moral question posed by the borrowings played the principal role so far as he was concerned. ... The Erba-Urio problem is more than I can deal with. Old Percy Robinson has a vast knowledge of Handel and his works, but he is a man with but a single idea in his head.

church music "borrowings" may come into the picture. As referred to in my *Messiah* book (p. 75 f.) there seems to be a rather close contact between church music traditions and oratorio traditions in Handel's orbit. His first English oratorio (ca. 1720) followed closely after his Chandos Anthems and made use of various pieces from the Brockes Passion. His next move towards an oratorio tradition (1732) was based partly on the adaptation of the Coronation Anthems, and again of music from the Brockes Passion. And now in 1738 he was determined to put the music from the Funeral Anthem (1737) into one of his two new oratorios; first he tried with *Saul* and then ended up with making it the first part of *Israel in Egypt*. But apparently he had no more church music ready to put him on the track of the oratorio tradition as before. In this situation he may have resorted to the Erba *Magnificat*, knowing or not remembering about the real composer from a time far back. (Of course this explanation has to do only with "borrowing" as a principle of construction, not with the question of morals.)

Was Handel a plagiarist? I am afraid the question is too simplistic to allow for a direct answer. Plagiarists will normally be people of limited talent, trying to add to their reputation by the use of borrowed plumes. But it is impossible to place Handel in the category of such people, nor is it justified to try to "defend" him against alleged immorality through a reference to his passing illness. Most likely he didn't ask about the origin of the thematic material stored in his musical memory; in this respect he may have been more as if rooted in the sixteenth, not the seventeenth or eighteenth, century — not to speak of the nineteenth or twentieth. And he may perhaps have had a — not unfounded — superiority complex, an unshakable conviction of his power of doing wonders with seemingly unimportant music material. His way of handling other composers' works would call for moral disapproval in perhaps all other cases, but — Taylor forgive me — what a good piece of luck that Handel ignored it.

JENS PETER LARSEN
Copenhagen
April 1979

Handel and his Orbit

Handel and his Orbit

BY

P. ROBINSON, B.A. (Oxon.)

LONDON
SHERRATT & HUGHES
Manchester : 34 Cross Street
1908

PREFACE

THE title, " Handel and his Orbit," has been chosen as expressing with sufficient accuracy the scope of this book. It is in no sense a " Life of Handel," nor is it concerned, a few words excepted, with æsthetic criticism. The object is to discuss some points of biography or history, more particularly where Handel's work touches the work of other musicians. That some portion of the subject has a general interest may be believed when we find this question among those set to the boys at Eton, January, 1908 : " Discuss Handel's borrowings from other composers."

An attempt is made here to present the relevant facts in rather greater detail than has been done elsewhere. By " relevant facts " is not meant the quotation of parallel passages ; this has been accomplished handsomely and with good temper by Mr. Sedley Taylor ; but such facts as throw light on the circumstances, and such as may help towards the distinguishing between the genuine and the non-genuine borrowings.

I have not hesitated to draw the inference that Handel's use of other composers was perfectly open, in which case it falls into line with the procedure of Bach, Beethoven, Brahms, and many others ; the abatements under the heading of originality in each case become then a mere matter of accountancy. From the opposite conclusion, set forth, though with some hesitation, I think, by Mr. Sedley Taylor, I should not have strongly dissented, if his book had contained all that could be learnt on the topic. But his candid discussion would not claim, I believe, to be in any way exhaustive, and has left room for inquiries conducted, I hope, in the same spirit. One important difference is concerned with three works, frequently attributed to Erba, Urio, and Stradella respectively. According to the evidence now available—and only with evidence, as interpreted by scholarship, which is another name for experience, need we concern ourselves—it would appear that these compositions should be regarded, the "Urio" with practical certainty, the others with sufficient confidence, as early works of Handel himself.

This particular subject was provisionally, and quite imperfectly, treated in an article in the International Musical Society's "Sammelbände" (July—September, 1907); for permission to make use of this I am indebted to the Society's courtesy. Of course, for all that is here advanced I alone am responsible.

My deep and constant obligation to the work of the late Doctor F. Chrysander will be apparent throughout the book. Not his industry alone, but also the conspicuous ability by which that industry was directed, should always command grateful recognition. But not even the work of a Gibbon can be final; we must supplement, we must rectify.

Large use has been made of a method recognised and employed by Dr. Chrysander (see below, p. 131), and by most serious critics. The principles have been sketched in Chapter XV. of the present book, and I may be permitted to refer here to an article, " Handel's influence on Bach," which appeared in the *Musical Times,* July, 1906. Turning over Handel's 1704 *Passion* I was reminded, by a phrase in it, of Bach's *Passion according to St. John.* On comparison I found also a number of slight resemblances, too trivial to be called borrowings, yet occurring in such a sequence that it was practically impossible to believe accident responsible for all. And I found subsequently that the text of the chorale " Durch dein Gefängniss " (" Thy bonds, O Son ") in Bach's *Passion* was throughout its six rhymed lines identical, but for one small word, with the text of an aria in Handel's *Passion,* the author of which was Postel of Hamburg. Again, in the article reproduced as an Appendix

(p. 189), for permission to insert which I am very grateful to Messrs. Novello and Company, the results were reached through the same principles, from resemblances dismissed at first as accidental. These things have a bearing on the main inquiry, as showing how easily evidence may be overlooked by excellent scholars, whose memory does not serve them at the proper season.

Of course, the strongest arguments are of no avail against convictions based on style, especially when, as in the present case, the objections seem never to have been formulated in detail. That which a man could not have written he could not have written despite the most over-whelming circumstantial evidence, despite any number of autographs, signed, erased and corrected. Recently Dr. Ernest Walker (*History of Music in England*, p. 207) pronounced " He is my God " (*Israel*) bad and un-Handelian, and fifty years ago Dr. H. J. Gauntlett (*Notes and Queries*, April 9, 1859) contrasted this same chorus with " The Lord shall reign " (*Israel*). Dr. Gauntlett pointed out the consecutive fifths : " Mark the stiffness and labour in all this, and then marvel at the masterly power of the other—the freedom, the constant movement and figure so determined to be obtained and so cleverly consummated." Dr. Walker, as I understand him, means "bad " in the technical sense ; and did Dr. Gauntlett agree with him ? Oh ! no ; that glowing eulogium is bestowed on the technique of " He is my God "; the consecutive fifths, the stiffness and labour belonged to the real Handel.

Mr. Fuller-Maitland (*Oxford History*, iv. 89) suggests that Handel honestly mistook the " Erba " *Magnificat* for a work of his own. The similarity of style was thus so strong as to deceive the very elect. The only modification required, then, is that Handel's sense of style was not here at fault.

My warm thanks are due to those who have furnished me with information and assistance of various kinds; to

Dr. Henry Watson, of Manchester, above all; to Signor Francesco Pasini of Milan; to Monsieur Julien Tiersot of Paris; to Sir Walter Parratt, Master of the King's Music, etc.; to Mr. W. Barclay Squire, of the British Museum; and to many others.

P. Robinson.

Manchester, *Sept.* 8, 1908.

It should be added that the monthly journal and the quarterly magazine of the International Musical Society are cited here as " Z. I. M. G." and " S. I. M. G."; that by " Chrysander " I mean the biography of Handel (in German) by Dr. Chrysander; that by " Spitta " I mean the life of Bach by Dr. Spitta in its English translation (1899); and that references to Otto Jahn's life of Mozart are to the English translation.

The chronological table at p. 216 may be found of service for reference.

CONTENTS

CONTENTS

CONTENTS

CHAPTER I.

HANDEL'S INFLUENCE.

IT was Franz Liszt who likened Handel to Homer. 'One cannot be always praising Homer,' wrote he, with polite deprecation of the too insistent enthusiasm of Handel's admirers. Of late this attitude, in itself not altogether unreasonable, has shown certain symptoms of development, in Great Britain, if nowhere else. Praise rarely isues from the lips of many who would claim to be reckoned among the most exquisitely framed of music's torch-bearers. When Handel's works are performed, a certain meed is, no doubt, accorded; but the exuberance of enthusiasm is sternly repressed, and in the intervals he is little mentioned, or mentioned but to lay stress on his defects. And, in so far as this represents a purely aesthetic judgment, it is useless to cavil. Assail the ghost of Hamlet's father with the most finely-tempered of Andrea Ferraras, and what will you accomplish? It is, as the air, invulnerable. Moreover, these critics may be exceptionally well qualified to judge; indeed, the imputation is seldom disclaimed.

But this reserved attitude is frequently justified on the ground of historical knowledge, or on general critical principles. This is not unfortunate, for, helpless though we become, when the question concerns differences of taste, in matters of history it may always be possible to reach agreement, while critical principles fairly invite examination of their validity or consistency. Some outstanding historical questions form the main subject of the present inquiry, and will be dealt with later in detail. But a preliminary discussion of some minor points may not be superfluous, and indeed may be found of equal general interest. A number of prevalent criticisms will be garnered—I fear after a slightly desultory fashion.

I.

There is a halo of criminality frequently affixed to what, at first sight, seems a purely involuntary offence. Handel, the allegation runs, exercised a repressing effect on English music, delayed until these happier days the genesis of that school, which will be esteemed hereafter among the chief glories of England. And this he did, not in the legitimate exercise of the influence which great artists have always possessed over contemporaries and successors, but in some subtle, not easily defined, but for all that exceedingly improper manner. After his death he still hovered, like a vampire, over his victims, and there would he be hovering even now, companioned by Mendelssohn, but for the efforts of sundry heaven-sent and high-minded deliverers.

If a defence may be attempted, one may urge that not a single potentially great composer in Handel's lifetime has yet been dragged from obscurity. This is allowed even by those who feel the injury most keenly. The crime, then, is a crime of the dead hand. Yet are we seriously invited to hold Handel responsible for what other people, over whom he cannot possibly have exercised any sort of control, chose to do, or omit to do, after his death? If subjects for whipping are wanted, why not fix on Burney, or Arnold, or some other of that band, which revived Handel's works, after they had been long cast aside, to use Burney's own phrase, 'as lumber'? The saddle seems to be wrongly attached; the whole charge smacks of transcendentalism; nay, if one closely considers the matter, it adds a 'new terror to death.'

Still, the result of Handel's innocent exertions may have been harmful. Though he himself changed slowly and reluctantly from opera to oratorio, and, in so doing, gave the English of his time a form of art, for which they showed a slightly greater affection, this affection might, but for him, have been quiescent. If England really was in evil case, the fact should not be blinked. Yet wailing should be proportioned to the outrage. Did it really matter one whit, if so many English composers turned out bad oratorios rather than bad operas or bad symphonies? Would they have stood much on the manner of their deaths—the dagger or the bowl of poison? Dispassionately viewed, oratorio is a highly meritorious form of art, and history lends no support to the view that other excellent forms were at any time banished from England's shores. On the contrary, Italian opera—see Burney—had always its vogue; for operas in English we have Arne, Bishop, Benedict, Balfe; the symphonies of Haydn, the symphonies of Beethoven found a ready welcome in England.

So far from being narrow and insular, as is frequently asserted, England has been at all times broad and cosmopolitan; this can be discerned by any one, who will take the trouble to examine musical history, and compare the reception of imported music in England with that accorded to it in any country of the continent. Our fault has rather been the opposite, of putting too low an estimate on native productions—none of them, perhaps, of the front rank, but bearing, in many cases, the imprint of real genius, with a well-marked vein of invention. And if, at the present day, composers have arisen, possessing the higher powers of flight, let us rather attribute this to personal causes, than to the removal of some mysterious ' obsession.' ' Soyons plus fiers!' If musical genius is visiting our shores more frequently, do not let us rush hotfoot to explain it away. Let us congratulate our composers on the possession, and ourselves on the recognition, of these ' strains of a higher mood.'

May I venture on a frivolous quotation from Gilbert's *Pygmalion and Galatea*?

> " I'm not aware that there is anything
> Extraordinary in my sitting down.
> The nature of the seated attitude
> Does not give scope for much variety."

Men of force, Handel, Bach, Beethoven, Wagner, always have influenced, and always will influence, the weaker composers. Over-enthusiasm will result in narrowness; but narrowness is not confined to this or that circle of adorers; it is an all-enfettering disease.

II.

It is often proclaimed that no school was founded by Handel, and this deficiency in posthumous pedagogy is thought very far from venial. I wonder, by the bye, whether painters, when standing before the Sistine Madonna, or the Monna Lisa at the Louvre, suddenly check their admiration to ask themselves nervously : 'But did Raphael, did Da Vinci found a school?' and then commence a search for their Crowe and Cavalcaselle. Do artists thus assess greatness? It seems to be a method that makes for discomfort.

It will be observed that this charge has an appearance, which may be superficial, of discrepancy with the indictment presented above. If Handel left no school, of what school was the much-commiserated band of deceased oratorio-writers in England? However, Goldsmith, writing the year after Handel's death, tells us that Handel *did* found a school. 'Handel may be said as justly as any man, not Pergolese excepted, to have founded a new school of music . . . . . . He has left some excellent and eminent scholars, particularly Worgan and Smith.'* And if these composers left no lasting mark, shall candour censure Handel for their want of genius? 'No one can be taught faster than he can learn. The speed of the horseman must be limited by the power of his horse.' This dictum of Dr. Johnson is, I venture to think, of universal application.

Perhaps, however, the objection is but a clipped expression for the want of influence on other great composers

* Goldsmith. *Miscellaneous Essays.*

often imputed to Handel. By this is not meant, I imagine, the lack of admiration for him in the minds of his successors, if such lack has ever been observed. Certainly the well-considered opinions of great musicians are always entitled to high respect. Indeed, when fifty Beethovens with peculiarly wide sympathies, fortified by high general education, and starting without prejudice, shall, in their riper years ['We talked a great deal of nonsense in those days,' said Wordsworth of his youthful depreciation of Virgil *], after careful and repeated comparison of Handel's total output with that of forty other admired composers, have assigned him his place, their average opinion will probably not be far from that of 'high-judging Jove.' But by want of influence is meant, I think, such as leaves an impression on the aspirations or the style of other writers.

Probably no one will seriously propose this as the sole test of greatness. Had the works of Shakespeare been performed privately, when all other writers were absent, and had they, thereafter, been buried for countless aeons in some subterranean cabinet, he would still, in the end, have been reckoned among the greatest. And had his plays, though open to all the world, left no visible impress on the productions of meritorious successors—and really it is difficult to trace very much—even then, spite of all, we should not cold-shoulder the writer of *Macbeth*.

Again, when we attempt to apply this criterion, not indeed as the sole, but still as a very important element in right judgment, we are confronted with this difficulty. Great is Mozart, for he influenced Beethoven; great again is Beethoven, for he influenced Wagner; great once more is Wagner, for he influenced—here it is better to invent— for he influenced our esteemed contemporary, Signor Chiva Sano. So far so good; but suddenly the horrid

* J. R. Lowell.

doubt presents itself. 'Yes, but *is* Signor Chiva Sano great?' He cannot yet have influenced any successor (whose greatness, to be sure, must be equally problematical), and this doubt makes Wagner's position insecure, rendering equally disputable the claims of Beethoven and Mozart. We are forced into that continuous suspense of judgment, admired by the Stoics, until the end of all that is perishable, when those last in the chain shall receive judgment simply and solely on the merits of their actual compositions. But if we shall be driven in the end to the actual works for the sole criterion, and as we are forced to apply it provisionally to contemporaries, would it not serve also for those who are dead? It seems at least clear that this 'influence' test should be assigned a very modest lot in life; it should serve at most for a small make-weight, to tip the balance, when there is otherwise equality. Further, its incidence fluctuates. In the eighteenth century it might have placed Handel above Bach; in the nineteenth Bach above Handel; in the twentieth what prophet may tell?

III.

Though rejected as a touchstone of genius, the influence of Handel on the course of music may still furnish an interesting subject for inquiry. Yet a difficulty meets us at the threshold. Limit music to half-a-dozen outstanding composers in a century, and suppose the selected company uninfluenced except by each other—a method to which lecturers naturally incline, that their audiences may have tangible points to grasp—and your task will be simple. But it will not do. Mozart was not primarily the musical son of Haydn; Beethoven was not primarily the musical son of Mozart. Were we to liken the fabric of music to a coral reef, in which the hosts of the labourers are all equal, this, no doubt, would be an exaggeration in the opposite direction; and yet of these countless labourers every accurate estimate must take some cognisance. We must remember that the 'Mozartian' style was by no means a style inherited from Haydn, but was, in large measure, the common possession of Haydn's contemporaries. We must not forget Jommelli and Paisiello, Gluck and Piccinni, Gossec and Grétry. We must bear in mind that the symphony, the quartet, the sonata form, were not the creations of Haydn, though finding in him, in their earlier days, their most accomplished champion. They who have a taste for forming 'royal lines'—perhaps an overrated form of amusement—will find the multitude so great as almost to vie with those on the scimitar of Saladin in Scott's *Talisman*, 'ten millions of meandering lines.'

Had Haydn never seen the light, Mozart would still have written symphonies and quartets—his own father wrote symphonies—in a style very similar to that of his existing works. But, on the whole, they might not have been quite so good; and this, not so much because of the details of technique, which Mozart may have learnt from Haydn, as because of the incentive, which Haydn's achievements supplied to his generous mind. And so too Beethoven, while owing something to Mozart in style and the arts of orchestration, which he might not so quickly or so completely have learnt elsewhere, though many others were working on similar lines, probably found in the actual beauty of Mozart's works his chief stimulus. Let us avoid being too material. Consider which man gave the greatest impulse to Beethoven's personality, Mozart, Napoleon, Handel, or Goethe. Or rather let us not consider a question to which no possible answer can be returned. Beethoven himself might have been quite unable to decide. In some moods he would represent himself as having learnt nothing from Haydn; at other times he might have been content to acknowledge a certain obligation. It is a wise composer that knows his own father. From those we are busily depreciating we may be learning

more than from those who have our constant good word.
For this reason, though it seems worth while to mention
some apparent illustrations of Handel's influence, there is
no desire to lay particular stress on them.   They have just
as much, just as little value, as other illustrations.

IV.

What reasons can be given, let us ask in the first place,
what reasons can be given for supposing that events did
not run their normal course in Handel's case?   Here was
a composer, whose first opera, *Almira,* achieved a great
success at Hamburg, a success which it seems to have fully
deserved; who visited Italy about 1707, and was received,
the country through, with enthusiasm, making a deep
impression, not only with his operas, church music, and
cantatas, but also by his skill on the harpsichord and
organ; who repeated in England with his *Rinaldo* (1711)
the triumphs of his *Almira* at Hamburg, and his *Agrippina* at Venice; whose *Leçons,* after circulating privately,
were issued in 1720, were reprinted in Holland, Germany,
France, and Switzerland, and proved the most popular
harpsichord music of the earlier part of the eighteenth
century.   Is it likely that all this happened, without an
impress being left on his contemporaries and juniors?
Would Italy wonder and forget?

When Handel was at Naples in 1708, Porpora was 22,
Vinci 18, Leo 14 years old.   These were the leading repre-
sentatives of that Italian band, which did so much to
displace the school of counterpoint, and enthrone the
harmonic style.   Leo instructed Jommelli, Porpora was the
teacher of Haydn.   Did the presence of the great Saxon
at Naples, where all that was distinguished vied to do him
honour, leave these young Neapolitans entirely unaffected?
According to 'Riemann' (s.v. Porpora), Handel congratulated Porpora on his *Berenice,* produced at Rome in 1710,
and though the details seem to require correction, the

story may rest on some foundation. Leo produced Handel's *Rinaldo* at Naples in 1718. Now it is true that Handel clung tenaciously to the contrapuntal style through-out life; yet there were always occasional incursions into harmonic methods. The later Italians expressed their incredulity to Burney as to Handel's use of iterated notes in his accompaniments,* yet we find it already in the *Nisi Dominus* (1707), the particular air being the lovely ' Cum dederit dilectis suis somnum ' (' For so he giveth his beloved sleep '), with its interesting resemblance to ' Mein Jesu, gute Nacht ' (' Lord Jesus, rest in peace ') of Bach's *St. Matthew Passion.* Out of the many examples of comparative modernity in different ways two may be men-tioned; the song 'Astro clemente ' in the cantata *O ! come chiare e belle* (Rome, 1708), and ' Dell' aquila l'artigli ' in *Aci* (Naples, 1708)—but indeed from *Aci* it is difficult to make a choice. The *Salve Regina* and the *Silete venti,* probably written at Rome or Naples, exhibit a greater leaning than would be generally anticipated towards the sacred style associated with the name of Pergolesi (1710— 1736 ?).

It is, I do not say likely, but at least possible that some of these things were known to the younger Neapolitans, and that they fastened on them, while rejecting the sterner parts of Handel's work. We may remember how Tenny-son was attracted by the less characteristically Miltonic parts of Milton :—

" Me rather all that bowery loneliness,
    The brooks of Eden mazily murmuring,"

Were we again to suggest that certain parts of the *Leçons* (1720), such as the preludes, or airs with variations, had some influence in helping on the ' galant ' style of harpsi-

* Illustrations of this are to be found in ' Comfort ye ' (*Messiah*), and, more markedly, in *Saul*, ' O Lord, whose mercies numberless.' The song which aroused the scepticism was the great ' Se possono tanto ' (*Poro*, 1730).

chord or clavier writing, we should suggest something at least incapable of disproof. Wagenseil of Vienna (1715—1788) was a great admirer of Handel, as Burney tells us;[*] indeed a copy of the ' Harmonious Blacksmith ' air, which he made, seems to have originated the idea that he was its actual composer.[†] Porpora, as we know, was Haydn's teacher at Vienna, and through him, we are told, Haydn was introduced to Wagenseil and Gluck. Well attested again is the admiration of Domenico Scarlatti (Nov. 1, 1685[‡]—1757) for Handel; when his own playing was praised, he would mention Handel's name, and cross himself; it is even added that through him Handel was long held in high esteem in Spain, though hardly anything of his music can have been known.[§] It was not till about 1730 that Domenico Scarlatti published his first work. Traces of his influence appear to be found in Beethoven.

V.

Passing by the tale of Hasse's refusing at first to write against Handel, and merely noting that C. H. Graun, the composer of the well-known *Der Tod Jesu,* made his début as a singer at Brunswick in Handel's *Ottone,* let us approach the greater names. For J. S. Bach not only have we traditional testimony of his admiration, but palpable proofs of his study (see Appendix, p. 189). Of most of Bach's works the dates are subject to doubt, and we are

[*] ' Tour in Germany,' i, 330.

[†] Dr. W. H. Cummings has shown that this was impossible, Wagenseil having been born in 1715. It can scarcely be doubted, moreover, that the air was developed by Handel from ' Mi dà speranza al core' in *Almira*—see ' Musical Times,' February 1906.

[‡] E. J. Dent. *Alessandro Scarlatti.*

[§] Chrysander, i, 229. It is interesting to find that the chief of the early Swedish school, Roman, was a pupil of Handel's. See Herr Niemann, ' S.I.M.G.,' v, 93 &c.

seldom sure whether what we possess is the original or a revised version. It is likely that prior to 1713, when he visited Handel's birthplace, Halle, and perhaps obtained his copy of *Almira,* he had advanced far in the development of that philosophic or religious melancholy, which supplies one of his chief claims to honour; but in many other directions his progress seems to have been comparatively slight. In addition to a concerto and cantata Bach possessed, it is recorded, a copy of Handel's second *Passion* (*circa* 1716). In the light of these facts it is difficult to see why Handel should not be regarded as filling towards Bach a position in some degree analogous to that occupied by Haydn in relation to Mozart. No doubt the extent of the obligation must be largely a matter of opinion. Textual obligations can be measured. When we find in Marlowe :—

" Was this the face that launch'd a thousand ships,"

and in Shakespeare (*Troilus and Cressida,* ii, 2, 82) :—

" Whose price hath launched above a thousand ships,"

we see the debt in the one line. But on the larger question, the interaction of mental and spiritual natures, we can only make conjectures.

Gluck told Burney that he owed everything to England, which he visited in 1745. Mr. Newman and Mr. Fuller-Maitland are inclined to dismiss this as a piece of unmeaning politeness, and, to be sure, the expression must have been exaggerated. A second story that Gluck was much indebted to Rameau, Handel, and Arne, is also discredited, and yet the introduction of Arne's name rather points to the story as originating with Gluck; who was likely to bring Arne into a mere invention ? However let us turn to Michael Kelly's well-known tale (*Reminiscences,* i, 255) :

" One morning after I had been singing with him, he

[Gluck] said 'Follow me upstairs, Sir, and I will introduce you to one, whom all my life I have made my study and endeavoured to imitate.' I followed him into his bedroom, and opposite to the head of the bed saw a full-length portrait of Handel in a rich frame. 'There, sir,' said he, 'is the portrait of the inspired master of our art; when I open my eyes in the morning I look upon him with reverential awe, and acknowledge him as such, and the highest praise is due to your country for having distinguished and cherished his gigantic genius.' "

This picture, it will be noticed, really cannot be explained away. Either the whole story is a baseless concoction of Kelly's—and we have not the slightest ground for such a judgment—or it must be accepted in substance as it stands. These three accounts united form a rampart that cannot be scaled. Gluck must have admired Handel immensely, and thought his own obligations to him and to England very considerable.

It may be a little difficult to trace much result in the works of Gluck, at least for a long time, though a certain advance in dramatic and representative power is credited to him, while Marx traces Handelian influence in *Tetide* (1749).* But the memory of an ideal may survive for fifteen years; throughout this interspace Gluck may have been fully alive to the merits of the style adopted later, and yet have been insufficiently in earnest to initiate a crusade. The advent of Calzabigi with his libretto of *Orfeo,* coupled with a certain change in public taste, would transform speculation into action. And if we inquire for the probable fertilising works, we come quickly to those produced just before Gluck's arrival in England (1745)—to *Semele* (1744), and *Hercules* (1745). These were dramas, given, it is true, without action, but still on the stage of a theatre; indeed, *Semele* was sometimes

* Newman. *Gluck and the Opera,* p. 33.

spoken of as an English opera.* Here we find the choruses, the dramatic scenas, the characterisation, in addition to the harmony between words and music, which sounds through nearly all Handel's work.† And had Gluck required anything foreign, to rouse from its slumber that warmth of tone, which he superadded to the grace of his contemporaries, to a greater extent, perhaps, than Haydn or Mozart, in such things as the dance-music and opening vistas of *Alcina* (1735), or the minuets in *Berenice* and *Ariadne,* this richer note might have reached his ear. The *Ariadne* minuet would assail him from every barrel-organ. As we shall see later, the abuses against which Gluck put on his armour were not rife in Handelian opera.

Of Haydn there is preserved an utterance to Shield, after hearing 'The nations tremble' in *Joshua,* that 'he was perfectly certain that only one inspired author ever did, or ever would, pen so sublime a composition.' Whether there is any good authority for the story that the *Creation's* libretto was originally prepared for Handel, I am uncertain; but it seems established that Haydn thought the *Creation* his own greatest achievement, and the filiation is equally beyond controversy.

Mozart was tardy in feeling Handel's spell. In 1777, at Mannheim, he did not sit out the rehearsal of *The Messiah.* Indeed the Mannheimers in general voted the work old-fashioned, and much preferred the more modern charms of Abt Vogler. And here let us remark parenthetically on the singular good luck of some of these old-fashioned works. They are for ever at the edge of that whirlpool that is

* Mainwaring's Catalogue. *Acis* was also called an opera.

† Some exceptions there are, no doubt, as Dr. Walker (*History of Music in England*, p. 197) has rightly urged. Yet the example selected by Dr. Walker from *Joshua* is not too felicitous. The lively music, that will not fit the melancholy lines quoted, yet does no violence to its actual yoke-mate, the couplet :

> 'Or who will not on Jordan smile,
> Releas'd from bondage on the Nile?'

to engulf them and hide them for ever in the haunts of the kraken, and yet they blunderingly evade taking the final fatal plunge. *The Messiah* and *Elijah* have to my certain information been dead these twenty-five years, or as good as dead, so dead, at least, that there is no more life left in them, and yet, somehow, like Lord Chesterfield, they 'don't choose to have it known' publicly. Perhaps Mozart preserved *The Messiah* at a critical moment by adding instrumentation to this and several more of Handel's compositions. In a letter of 1782 he praised the fugues of 'Handel and Bach'; he even wrote a suite in the style of their days. Rochlitz said that Mozart was as familiar with the works of Handel as if he had been all his life director of the Ancient Concerts in London. "Of all of us," said Mozart, according to the same authority, "Handel knows best how to produce great effects; where he desires to produce it, he 'crushes like thunder.' Even if—after the fashion of his time—he is trudging along, we still find something in it." How far the *Requiem* and other later works were influenced by Handel must remain a matter of opinion. In the first movement of the *Requiem* we find a fragment of chorale melody, which had been used in Handel's *Funeral Anthem;* in the second the fugue subject (or subjects) is found also in Handel's *Joseph.*

Beethoven's admiration for Handel is well-known. Though nurtured on Mozart he had a preference for the Saxon, while Sebastian Bach ranked third in his esteem.*

* Dr. Walker (*History of Music in England,* p. 205) remarks on Beethoven's limited knowledge of his predecessors, and the remark seems quite fair, though its application may be extended, with equal fairness, to the *obiter dicta* of other composers. That eulogium, for instance, by Schumann, cited at the head of 'Grove's' article on Bach, displays little historical knowledge, apart from its ungrateful form. And let it be remembered, that with Bach's '48,' to question whose plenary inspiration seems nowadays little short of a hanging matter, Beethoven was familiar from his boyhood. At such times as he praised *The Messiah* even more than the '48,' I suppose he was 'not a musician,' to use a favourite and blighting, though perhaps a trifle crude, form of expressing disagreement.

He 'loved' Handel, as he told an English lady, whose letters
was printed in the *Harmonicon*, December, 1825. 'Handel
is the greatest composer that ever lived.' . . . 'I would
uncover my head, and kneel down at his tomb.' These
utterances were taken down at once, and printed in the
Harmonicon, January, 1824, three years before Beethoven's
death. We also find a story that, when near to his end,
he turned over Handel's scores with delight. 'That is
the truth—das Wahre' was his comment. Once we find
him looking at the paths trod by Handel. His friend,
C. Bernard, had constructed an oratorio-libretto, called
Victory of the Cross; and Beethoven, after completing the
Choral Symphony, entered seriously into the scheme of
setting this text. However, the scheme came to nothing.
It has often been observed how scanty are the traces of
Handel's direct influence in Beethoven's scores, in spite
of this admiration. The styles the two had inherited were
quite dissimilar. The influence was of a deeper and really
vital character, as Raphael might have been more vitally
influenced by the statues of Michael Angelo than by the
pictures of Perugino, or as Goethe was deeply penetrated
by the spirit but not by the outward forms of Shakespeare.

Weber, in his discontent with Beethoven's 4th Symphony, lamented the decay of clearness and force, spirit
and fancy 'like those of Gluck, Handel, and Mozart.'*
However, this was an utterance of youth.

Schubert, according to report, learnt to know Handel
towards the close of his life. 'I now see,' said he, 'how
much I have to learn,' and applied himself again to study.

To Spohr we find his librettist Rochlitz writing the hope
that he will do for his time what had been done for a
past age by Handel.†

---

* Sir George Grove. *Beethoven and his Nine Symphonies*, p. 102.

† Herr Rychnovsky. 'S.I.M.G.,' v, 266.

It is needless to expand on the subject of Mendelssohn. It is curious to find him recommending to his sister for performance the psalm *Dixit Dominus* (1707), as it had not then been published, according to Mr. Rockstro's list, and the only MS. in England, so far as appears, is the autograph.   Were there German copies?

Schumann on February 14th, 1851, writes to his intended librettist Pohl : ' I suppose you know Handel's *Israel in Egypt?*   That is my ideal of a choral work.'   The proposed oratorio, *Luther*, remained unwritten, but Schumann lets us know his ideas as to the treatment.   Mere narrative or reflections to be avoided as much as possible, and the dramatic form always to have the preference. The oratorio should be ' a distinctly popular one, which peasant and citizen could understand.' . . . ' I should endeavour to keep my music in this spirit, and accordingly anything but artificial complicated and contrapuntal, but simple, impressive, and depending for effect mainly on rhythm and melody.' (June 25th, 1851.)

It is not well-known, by the bye, that Schumann preferred the *St. John Passion* of Bach to the *St. Matthew* (Letters to Hauptmann, April 2nd, 1849, May 8th, 1851). The *St. John* is more powerful and poetical.   ' I think it [the *St. Matthew*] contains some shallow parts and is altogether inordinately long.   But the other—how condensed, how full of genius, especially the choruses, and what consummate art !'

Liszt (Letter to Hauptmann, September 25th, 1855) spoke of the Coronation Anthem, *Zadok the Priest,* as a glorious ray of Handel's genius, ' grand comme le monde.'   He was also much interested in *L'Allegro* as an important contribution to imitative music.

Chopin's friend, Hiller, translated Handel's *Deborah* in 1834, and provided additional accompaniments for a performance at Aix-la-Chapelle. Whether Chopin shared Hiller's enthusiasm I do not know, but he was anxious to accompany him from Paris, and raised the necessary funds by selling the E flat waltz for 500 francs. This story and the utterances of Liszt are merely added as having a certain interest.

Observe then, that while Haydn, Mendelssohn, and Spohr followed in Handel's footsteps, Beethoven, and even Schumann, his devotion to Bach notwithstanding, were preparing to do the same. In its vital force Handel's influence reached Haydn, Mozart, and Schubert, if we may not add Schumann, only towards the close of their careers. Had it come earlier, or had the lives of Mozart and Schubert been extended, what new births might have astonished us! But alas! 'Atropos for Lucina came.' That, which might have been, was not; many a fair statue will wait till the crack of doom, imprisoned beyond our ken in the marble.

CHAPTER II.

CONVENTIONALISM AND OPERA.

I.

A FAVOURED criticism tells us that Handel made no advance in the art of music. Those who allow themselves in such reflections do not imply, I think, that Handel did not give us new conceptions, more noble and more beautiful than had appeared in the seventeenth century, nor again that he did not first show, in ample development, the 'grand' style in music—a very different thing, be it noted, from the 'Handelian' style. These are things of the spirit, but we are to concern ourselves here with mechanical, material, formal considerations; with such merits as were possessed by the Frenchman Voiture, who exhibited 'an inexhaustible variety of forms, which he applies to a monotonous sterility of ideas.' Descending, then, to these quasi-prosaic matters, we may ask whether the reflection be well-based. To take form in its larger aspects, was not the development of oratorio by Handel entirely parallel to the development of symphony by Haydn, and had it not some analogy at least to the development of music-drama by Wagner? It represents surely a larger stride than we find Beethoven, Bach, or Brahms essaying. What large change did Bach introduce in the 'Passion,' the cantata, the suite, the concerto? His *Passions* are built on the lines, sufficiently conventional, of many previous *Passions*. In the suite, it is confessed by Spitta, Handel was decidedly the more enterprising, if such trifles may be dignified with the name of enterprise. Yet, strangely enough, this merit is turned into a reproach; here the correct thing was, it should seem, 'stare super antiquas vias,' to make no forward movement.

Or let us turn to narrower aspects. Take the fugue. Here Handel was admittedly freer than Bach. Time after time you will find him quitting the prescribed route, if only thereby extra beauty may be captured. In the use of harmonic methods he is unquestionably by far the more liberal, and Mr. Fuller-Maitland brings to the light his comparative modernity in orchestration; the interchange and contrast of the tones of different instruments (*Oxf. Hist.*, iv, 132). Whether the reproach of 'conventionality,' of adherence to old forms and methods, be very terrible, may be doubted, yet in these large matters of form it should attach to Bach rather than to Handel. Mr. Fuller-Maitland points with justice to Bach's curious clinging, till late in life, to a Scarlattian formula—the enunciation of the first phrase in an aria, much as a preacher announces his text, and the following it by an instrumental interlude, before the real discourse begins. Handel after his early days made sparing use of this formula. Another convention loved by Bach was the inverting of the theme of a gigue in a second section.

Those *rococo* 'divisions,' which meet us in the scores of Bach and Handel, and which seem, and indeed are, so easy to write, should perhaps not be termed 'conventional'; at least the occasion and extent of their introduction was a matter of choice, or they might be omitted entirely. They are really ornate modes of expressing the evolution of emotion, which have fallen into disuse; nowadays we fly rather to polyphonic chromatic passages. It is curious how similar instrumental passages, which seem to stand on the same intellectual footing, do not appear equally old-fashioned. I have taken down a cantata of Bach's, and turned to the first song. Here at bars 24—26 a long and apparently empty 'division'*

---

* As a rule Bach's 'divisions' are slightly more sinuous than those of Handel; German rather than Italian; of course, they were equally easy to write.

shows its face. Yet in the opening chorus of the same cantata ('How brightly shines yon star of morn') at bars 24—28 is a still longer and apparently equally empty passage for the instruments, which would irritate less, I suspect, an irritable modern critic. I have said 'apparently empty,' meaning that they would be empty if detached from the context; but, of course, in the airs of a great composer, bating those moments when he is writing with his left hand, they may be just what was wanted to make the whole composition flawless. To decide when a particular passage is in its place, we must have acuteness, discrimination, a ready and flexible sympathy. 'Qui respicit ad pauca, de facili pronuntiat.' Occasion does not serve just now to take the mete-wand through the whole of the airs of Bach and Handel.

That prolific composers like Handel and Bach should fall into personal mannerisms was only to be expected; not even Shakespeare is entirely free from this failing. It is rather surprising that Bach's use of the minor 7th, pointed out by Mr. H. H. Statham in his *My Thoughts on Music,* has not attracted more attention. It makes an early appearance in many of Bach's most popular arias, *e.g.,* 'Bereite dich' ('Prepare thyself'), and the slumber aria in the *Christmas oratorio,* and in 'Schlummert ein' from the cantata *Ich habe genug.* Or take the *St. Matthew Passion,* and examine a portion, say those numbers in the key of G. In the first, a chorus, the first two bars are more or less preparatory, so that the appearance of the F natural in the soprano part is delayed till bar 4. But in the aria 'Ich will dir' ('Lord to thee') the second quaver of the second bar of the voice-part is F natural. In the chorus 'Er ist des Todes' ('He is of death') the last crotchet of bar 1 (soprano part) is F natural. In the remaining number in G, the bass aria, the F natural waits till bar 3 of the voice-part. In our second example (the air) that tie between bars 2 and 3, and that F G in the instruments in bar 3, are surely ridden pretty hard in Bach's works. It would not be worth while to point out these things—of course the number might be much increased—if it had not been strangely claimed for Bach that he was quite free from mannerisms.

Handel's style is, of course, less chromatic than that of Bach, and it is very likely that the latter was the first to use a certain number of harmonies and progressions. It is difficult, indeed, to be sure in these matters. A number of Bach's predecessors were fond of experimenting, Buxtehude, for instance, and J. C. Bach.* Perhaps the necessity of varying their chorales inclined them to make trial of fresh harmonies. J. S. Bach was well placed for the purposes of study; he was 'seated in hearing of a hundred streams.' His chief distinction is, perhaps, rather the longer persistence in the less simple harmonies, and the slight, though tolerably obvious extension of well-understood principles. Purcell and Scarlatti were harmonists of scope, and Handel himself was no novice. [A few specimens of harmonies a little out of the beaten track are shown in Note A, p. 201.]

Turning to minor points we find Professor Prout scenting a foreshadowing of sonata form in a couple of clavier preludes by Bach—Prelude 29 of the '48,' and a Prelude (with Fughetta) in G. With a great deal of good will a resemblance may, perhaps, be hammered out. Still, with far less difficulty, we can discern the sonata form of the more modern and freer type, without the repetition and without strict verbatim reproduction, in the first movement of the overture to Handel's *Saul*. Here, far more clearly than in the examples from Bach, are to be traced the first subject, the 'bridge' passage, and the second subject. Yet pure accident may be suspected, rather than the 'prophetic soul dreaming on things to come.'

Some first-knowns have been credited to Handel; the

* Spitta.

first choral recitative ('He sent a thick darkness,' *Israel*);
the first scenic quintet or sextet, *Flavio;* the first use of
$\frac{5}{8}$ time, *Orlando;** the first introduction of cadenzas in
concertos; perhaps an anticipation of the scheme of
Beethoven's Choral Symphony.   Very likely research will
disprove, or has already disproved, these priorities; we
are always in danger of bringing home wheelbarrows as
new improvements.   Bach has received much praise for
marking off the words of Christ from those of other
speakers in the *St. Matthew Passion* (1729) by means of
a string-band accompaniment.   Yet others before him had
done the same, including Handel in his 1704 *Passion*.
'Bach, who anticipated nearly all modern harmonic progressions, was one of the first to use other chords of the
7th than that on the dominant in this manner' [*i.e.*,
without preparation], writes Professor Prout (*Harmony*,
Chap. xviii.).   This is, no doubt, true; however, we find
Handel already doing the same in the *Dixit Dominus*
(1707), first movement, bar 102.   Sir George Grove adduces
an early instance of abrupt commencement, the 7—5—4—2
chord in a cantata by Bach 'who seems to have anticipated
everything that later composers can do.'†   Turn to the
cantata *Partenza* (1708), and we shall find Handel opening
with a 7 sharp—4—2, the voice itself striking the sharp 7th
at the very first note; perhaps he regarded it as a puerile
conceit, and never cared to repeat it.   Such things, in
truth, put no terrific strain on the intellect.

It may be through the difficulty of finding words for the
essential things in music, that we not rarely find singled
out for particular praise that diminished 7th at the cry
'Barabbas' in Bach's *St. Matthew Passion;* the essence
of the feat not lying in the æsthetic felicity of the introduction, but in the marvellous brilliance of the bare idea.
Yet such brilliance seems well within the powers of a

---

* The air 'Si poco è forte' in *Berenice* is marked $^9/_8$.

† *Beethoven and his Nine Symphonies*, p. 4.

quite modest invention. Indeed, much of the praise bestowed on Bach seems by no means peculiarly happy in its conception. Writing fluently in eight, ten, fifteen parts is, no doubt, an attainment possible only to high mental power, even if, like Bach, we are a little autocratic in our treatment of the 'consecutive fifths' prohibition; but the ability can scarcely be deemed specifically musical. The stress sometimes laid on such things may recall Jane Austen's *Emma,* and the eulogium by Mrs. Elton : ' Wax candles in the schoolroom ! You may imagine how desirable ! ' ' Nine real parts, fugues ricercate, stretti maestrali ! You may imagine how desirable ! ' To Bach himself such things were probably but idle gauds. It has been observed that in the second part of the ' 48 ' the greater number of the fugues are written for no more than three voices; such small importance did he attach to mere complexity. Beethoven's views seem to have been very similar, if the words attributed to him were really spoken : ' Handel is the unrivalled master of all masters ! Betake yourselves to him, and learn to produce with such small means such mighty effects.' Bach's claims to veneration may be more securely rested on the many mighty and noble conceptions studding the spacious champaign of his fifty or more volumes. By taking these to our hearts, rather than by counting notes, or parts, or by observing that his style is chromatic—not a very difficult observation to make—shall we do him real honour. Teach the young student such inexpensive methods of appreciation, and what inducement do you give him to study Bach's works ? He will spontaneously trust his teacher's powers of simple enumeration. Meanwhile Bach ' laudatur et alget.'

II.

Let us turn to Handelian opera. According to rumour this was governed by the hide-bound set of rules, which the late Mr. Rockstro reproduced from a writer, or writers, who flourished later than Handel's day. Mr. Rockstro, himself, was careful to state that Handel never hesitated to break these rules, but this qualification, though not unimportant, is generally overlooked. Consequently we get remarkable statements, such as these :—

1. *There must be always six principal characters.* [Generally there are more than six characters altogether, yet it is seldom that in Handel's operas more than five can fairly be called principal characters. *Orlando* (1732) has but five characters in all. *Imeneo* (1740) has only five, and one of these, Argenio, has only one air throughout the work. *Amadigi* (1715), with its five nominal characters, goes further; Orgando has no air at all to sing, according to the existing score.]

2. *That the hero and principal singer must be an artificial soprano.* [Senesino, the hero of nearly half Handel's operas was a contralto; his successor, Carestini, was also a contralto.]

3. *That in each act each of the principal singers must sing at least one air.* [In *Teseo* neither Medea nor Teseo appears in the first act of all : Clizia, Arcane, and Agilea are absent from the second. Indeed, there is no character who sings an air in each of the five acts. In *Admeto* Hercules has no air to sing in Act ii. In Graun's *Montezuma* Cortes does not appear at all in Act i., though there are only three acts.]

4. *That no singer must sing two airs in succession.* [Broken in *Rodrigo,* in *Agrippina,* and everywhere throughout the series.]

5. *That no two consecutive airs must be of the same class;* there being five classes, the *aria cantabile,* the *aria di portamento,* the *aria parlante,* the *aria di bravura,* and the *aria di mezzo carattere,* with their numerous subdivisions and cross-divisions. Such things bring to mind Wordsworth's distinction of his smaller poems into those

poems 'founded on the affections,' 'poems of the fancy,' 'poems of the imagination,' and 'poems of sentiment and reflection,' as to which it has been traitorously revealed, that he himself was often puzzled to assign them aright. How nicely-dividing were those eighteenth-century giants! Did any text-book exist to teach these subtle distinctions to budding composers, or were they left, like little Isaac Newtons, 'wandering through strange seas of thought alone'? Was there a censor to reject the operas of the ignorant or the rebellious, and was there any possibility of appeal from his decision? Where are the passages in Burney, Marcello, or the all-embracing Mattheson, which throw light on these obscurities? Bold it may be, yet I will venture the opinion that neither Handel nor any composer of his time had ever heard one syllable of these rules; if I am mistaken, and they really did obtain, Handel, it is clear, was a St. George-like trampler on convention, a militant anti-Philistine.

The real operatic scheme was very simple, very natural, very unconventional. Your librettist constructed a plot with a reasonable number of characters, say five to nine; like Gluck's librettists, and like the average novelist, he generally steered his hero and heroine triumphantly through their perils.* You assigned to your best and most popular singers the best of your parts and as the bass has seldom been very popular, the bass usually came off rather scurvily. As the plot dealt with the fortunes of the principal characters, who can wonder that these principals appeared in nearly every act? You transacted your business in *recitativo secco*, adding instruments at some more impassioned moments, while, in the intervals of business, the characters gave voice to their sentiments in full-blown arias. Students of nature will have observed, with Rousseau, that two persons seldom talk at length together in real life, still less in perfect harmony; now, in

* Yet not always; *e.g.*, Graun's *Montezuma*.

our operas, these unnatural duets occur but rarely—there is none in *Agrippina*—and, where they occur, the hero and heroine are generally found to be expressing congenial and harmonious sentiments. Only by exception have trios and quartets any *locus standi;* but the characters generally join forces to sing their common sentiments at the end of the opera, or elsewhere. Choruses in the modern sense are rare; they were brought in occasionally as in *Alcina* and *Deidamia,* where bodies of men really have some right to be present; but the audiences of that day had no yearning to see twenty or thirty shoe-makers singing away lustily in the first act, not having the slightest inducement, to reappear as a troop of vocal brigands or melodious cuirassiers in Act ii.

Of course, some concessions to convention had to be made; instruments were not kept outside the stage-door. It was quite rare for the voice to sing absolutely without accompaniment; yet measure was observed for the most part, if Handel was sometimes sadly at fault. To the amount and elaboration of his orchestral writing strong-seeming objections were raised by Bononcini; however, it is difficult to determine where a line should be drawn.

It may be objected that such operas, though delightfully natural and unconventional, yet lack variety, and may in practice prove wearisome; nature suffices not for everything. And in this objection there may be some force; it might have been more judicious to thrust in a larger number of conventional duets, quartets, and choruses. Even the ballet, which rarely appears in Handel's scores, might be welcomed, if not carried to excess, ás in the operas of Gluck. Nay, those composers, who have followed Handel's lead in augmenting the orchestra, and giving it greater scope, have increased, I incline to think, ' the stock of harmless pleasure.' Nevertheless, if we take high ground, these continual concessions to convention have in them something disquieting; they incur the suspicion of being bids for popularity. Wagner, perhaps, felt this, and in his *Tristan and Isolde,* which is often reckoned his most mature work, cut down the choral and concerted music to a minimum. The orchestra at Bayreuth is placed out of sight; a thorough-going spirit of reform, a whole-hearted love of nature, might have placed it also out of hearing. However, this might be too quixotic, too Rousseau-ish.

From the minor absurdities Handelian opera seems to have been reasonably free. The airs, to take them as a whole, are introduced in the interstices of the action, and hardly ever interfere with it. In the *Magic Flute,* we may remember, Monostatos, after observing that there is a capital opportunity for snatching a kiss from the sleeping Pamina, cannot refrain from singing a vigorous aria—no lullaby—with the natural result that the Queen of the Night arrives in time to foil him. Absurdities like this are rarely, if ever, found in Handel's operas.

III.

We are sometimes given to understand that the singers, with the jealous requirements of their respective positions, dominated these operas. Here, at least, we escape from suspicion of conventionalism; the singers would make short work of the poor composer's plaint, that to insert a particular song here or there would introduce 'false relation' among his *cantabiles* and *parlantes*. But it is not clear that Handel studied the singers more than was reasonable; that is, more than composers and managers have had to study them in all ages, not excluding the present. Senesino and perhaps Carestini regarded him as a tyrant, and Cuzzoni, singing 'Falsa immagine' under threat of being hurled from the window, could hardly have felt that she was having it all her own way. The librettos of Zeno, Haym, and Metastasio, made some characters subordinate to others, and did not allow their

Rosencrantzes to have more to do than their Hamlets. Handel engaged his singers of different degrees of merit and standing, and allotted the parts in the natural way. He did not write a pathetic air, when the words or situation demanded an *aria di bravura,* whatever might be the personal tastes of the singer. Assuredly, on the score of congruence with the words and situation, his operatic music requires no apology; indeed, as Gervinus and Mr. R. A. Streatfield have pointed out, there are many instances of happy characterisation. That this congruence was at all uncommon in his time, I do not affirm. It is significant that Algarotti, who preached the reform of the opera in Gluck's day, wished to *go back* to the subservience of the musician to the poet, 'of Vinci [1690 —1730] to Metastasio.' *

IV.

The extensive use of the *da capo* form in the arias of Handel, Bach, and Scarlatti, cannot, it must be confessed, be acquitted of monotony. It would have been better, had there been more variety of form. Probably one of the reasons that recommended it to opera composers was the fact that the separate successful airs were frequently sung in private. Those of Handel were printed without the recitatives, sometimes in mere selections. For separate singing in the home or at private concerts, the *da capo* form was very convenient; the audience grasped the meaning of the first part more clearly on the repetition, in the varying and ornamenting of which the singer was expected to display his talent. Still, the practice produced monotony. On the other hand, the objection that the *da capo* form is undramatic fails to cleave the wand. The aria, whatever its structure, interrupts the action, and if inserted at an unsuitable place is always to be condemned.

* E. Newman. *Gluck and the Opera,* p. 233.

But we are dealing with the breathing-spaces in the march of the action, moments it may be, when the heroes and heroines escape the trammels of circumstance, and pour forth their settled souls. The question to be asked is, whether the repetition be psychological. Do we find in real life that after a full emotion or a pondering on one subject, a temporary deflection is made, at the conclusion of which we return to the first emotion or subject in its undiminished fulness? Surely this is the common every-day experience. If Chloris despise her lover at the hour of nine, she will despise him no less two minutes later. Tannhäuser yearns to be allowed to leave Venusberg; he is seduced, for the moment, to sing the praise of the goddess, but the first wish returns as potent and engrossing as ever : ' Goddess, let me fly.' Our settled moods are interrupted, but not easily banished. Now words and music are but the operatic time-vestures of these states of soul. When the mood returns in its completeness, why should the outward trappings suffer change? Gluck, at least, could not have perceived the inappropriateness; in his last great opera, *Iphigénie en Tauride,* he uses the form three times out of some nine or ten possible oppor-tunities.*

I have mentioned Bach's name, for I feel that he would scarcely have wished to escape criticism with the flimsy excuse that he never wrote an opera. He set quite a number of *dramme per musica*—an expression, be it remembered, often used to describe an opera—and in these dramas nearly every air exhibits the *da capo*. Neither Bach nor Handel seems ever to have conceived the slightest prejudice against the form, though some of Handel's later operas, *Serse,* for example, exhibit it less frequently.

---

* (1) 'Oh ! toi qui prolongeas mes jours.' (2) 'Dieux, qui me poursuivez.' (3) 'Ah ! mon ami.' In the last example the exact repetition is forsaken only to add one bar, introducing an ejaculation by Orestes. Otherwise we have in all three cases a verbatim repetition of words and music.

Perhaps I am wrong in supposing Mr. Fuller-Maitland
(*Oxf. Hist.*, iv, 44) suggests that Bach purposely avoided
the aria structure in the B minor *Mass,* being desirous of
departing from the 'conventionalism of his time in every
way that was possible.' There can be no harm, anyhow,
in noting that the *da capo* air seems to have been avoided
generally in compositions of that class. It finds no place
in Bach's *Magnificat,* in Handel's *Te Deums,* in Leo's
Dixit Dominus, in the settings of the *Stabat Mater* by
Pergolesi and Astorga, to name some celebrated works of
the same class. It would rather seem that custom or
convention dictated the exclusion. On the preceding page
Mr. Fuller-Maitland's elucidation is a little disquieting.
He thinks there are signs that Bach did not consider
the Scarlattian formula, referred to on p. 19, 'worthy of
his most dignified and important work,' for in the *St.
Matthew Passion* there is only one example, and in the
St. John Passion only two, one being imperfect. But this
turns Bach into a sort of Ovid :—

> ' Video meliora, proboque ;
> Deteriora sequor.'

His virtue or artistic sense only served on important
occasions, and even in the *St. Matthew Passion* he was a
backslider in the last air.

It may have been Frederick the Great who had the
largest share in killing the vogue of the *da capo*. Hasse
had been displaying, like Handel in *Serse,* a leaning
towards the *cavatina;* and Frederick, in writing the libretto
of Graun's *Montezuma,* constructed most of his lyrics for
that form.* Subsequently Graun wrote comparatively
few *da capo* arias, and the decline became general, though
as noticed above, it was not completely banished, even in
1779.

* See the preface to the edition of *Montezuma* in the 'Denkmäler der
Tonkunst.' The date of this opera is 1755.

V.

The Recitative of Handel is frequently contrasted to its disadvantage with the 'expressive' Recitative of Bach and Purcell. Those prairie-like stretches, unillumined, when the eye peruses them, by the histrionic powers of the singers, and by the filling-up of the harpsichordist, do appear monotonous. Yet this question of Recitative is by no means easy. In connexion with Wagner's operas it is still a subject of debate. It was with eyes fully open that Handel rejected the 'expressive' pre-Scarlattian style. In some of his early works it peeps out to a certain extent, and it is significant that when he had occasion to revise such works later, the passages in question were eliminated or much modified (cf., *e.g.,* the two versions of the cantata *Sento là che ristretto*). That restlessness, not remote from jerkiness, with its *arioso* passages, was considered by Scarlatti, it would seem, unnatural and unsuited to opera; it appeared to transcend too far the boundaries of speech, nor could it produce the wished-for contrast with the aria. But Bach had not the same inducement to cultivate a more tranquil style. Generally speaking, he was not called upon to supply Recitative for conversations and plottings, but to words intended for edification, or for narratives like those in the *Passions,* where the words may be viewed as though transfigured. Had it been Purcell's and Bach's lot to set long opera-texts, they would have reflected that, as Lord Macaulay might have put it, we do not live in the days of Hilpa and Shalum. Instead of trying to foist expressiveness on the expansive vacuities of his librettists, and instead of lengthening the agony by such caracoling as is to be found in the scores of Bach and Purcell, Handel reserved himself for the really impassioned portions, and then, whether with or without stringed accompaniment, he generally produced something fine.

The methods of opera he continued in his dramatic

oratorios, produced, like the operas, on the stage of a
theatre. His librettists still gave him large expanses of
prosaic text, which did nothing but carry on the business.
The Messiah, Israel, L'Allegro, Alexander's Feast, are
exceptions, and in these the Recitative is not likely to
evoke much criticism. But in the majority we find tracts
of *recitativo secco,* such as confront us in the operas of
Mozart. If the librettists had noticed the futility of three-
fourths of their labours, they would certainly have earned
our gratitude. As it is, the pruning-knife is desirable,
and is usually applied. The plot may suffer a little in the
process, but, in any case, singers in evening wear cannot
easily produce the illusions of drama.

The direct comparison, then, of the Recitative of Handel
and Bach seems unprofitable. In its own sphere Bach's
Recitative, at its best, has, no doubt, high merit. True,
repetition cannot be avoided; the same phrases, the same
turns of melody, the same harmonies must frequently
recur. Perhaps it might be urged that the bulk of the
expressiveness merely pricks the skin; and that much the
same kind serves the turn of religious sorrow, religious
joy, compliments to patrons, and wrangles over coffee.
Spitta (ii. 445) has observed occasionally a lack of agreement between the words and the music, and attributed it
to the haste in composition, to which the autographs bear
witness. But it could not be expected that Bach should
always furnish something new or something great, small
though the amount of text to be set was in comparison
with that of the opera-writers. The labour would have
been quite disproportioned to the profit. Keiser arouses
our sympathy, when he tells us a piece of recitative may
cost as much headache as a whole aria.

For the *recitativo secco* it may be claimed that the
subservience of the musician to the dramatist is even
better preserved than in the later styles, wherein the singers
are 'cabin'd, confined, bound in' by the orchestra. A

nearer approach to nature cannot fairly be denied to the Handelian practice. No doubt, to those who regard opera as an entertainment primarily sensuous, the old-fashioned opera scheme is uninviting; it lacked variety both of form and orchestration, and above all it lacked theatrical tension —continuous nervous excitement, and frequent climaxes; the personages often move and act as calmly as though they were real people, nay normal and civilised beings; they plot as unemotionally as actual cabinet ministers or real anarchists. But the empyrean-scaling theatre can and does improve on real life; a chorus whose unstaged thoughts and actions would severally vary beyond calculation—some of them, perhaps, as indifferent to the larger issues as Goethe's nut-cracking Philine—will lend their ears with consentaneous and equal horror, and pour forth their indignation in precisely the same words at precisely the same time. 'When they do agree on the stage, their unanimity is wonderful!' And an excellent thing too! But do not let us therefore despise or misrepresent the inartificial simplicity of our forefathers.

VI.

No obstacle seems to hinder our regarding this old-fashioned opera as a vehicle, sufficient in the hands of the right man for the expression of high passion, of beauty, of dramatic and psychological truth. Danger there was, it is true. Just as, in less skilled hands, the Wagnerian music-drama may open the gates to flabby sentimentalism, boisterous convulsions, blatant imbecilities, or to a pandering to a virtuoso orchestra; so of these earlier opera-writers the vast majority could only have ploughed the sands. The combination of the qualities necessary for success in high serious plays is granted but to one or two in a generation; and to how many are allotted such powers as may bid defiance to all changes of language and taste? When, among tragic writers, we have named Aeschylus,

Sophocles, and Euripides, we must descend apparently to Shakespeare. And after Shakespeare? Are Corneille and Racine often staged outside France, or Schiller and Goethe outside Germany? It is difficult to be a great and ever-living dramatist, and these earlier composers suffered moreover from ill-conceived librettos, to our thinking. Not only was the structure faulty, but they contained what Dr. Johnson once called, too much 'Tig and Tirry.'* The composers suffered also from over-production; many brought out, on an average, two or three each year; while those of Gluck's serious dramas, which are now remembered, appeared at an average interval of three years. Nevertheless, when we say these earlier men suffered, we merely mean that in other conceivable circumstances some of them might have received higher commendation from musical historians. The remembrance of Leo, Vinci, Porpora, etc., depends practically (I do not say deservedly) on a song or two; and to a moral certainty the case would not have been altered, had any of them adopted by anticipation the later methods of Gluck. They had not that height of genius, which alone confers immortality on large works. And if songs from their operas were strung together on a light framework, forming a *pasticcio*—a procedure having, except for the presence of a framework, a certain resemblance to a 'Wagner Night'†—we need not grudge the people of those days an agreeable form of concert, or pity the composers, because a longer life was given to some fragment of their inspirations.

Am I wrong, by the bye, in imagining that, whereas *Iphigénie en Tauride* is the most theoretically perfect of Gluck's operas, and but the rudiments of right method are exhibited by *Orfeo*, the latter is quite as well-known, and quite as popular? Subject and felicity count for so

* Tigranes and Tiridates.
† It must be remembered that in most places the theatres were the only large concert-rooms.

much. Is it certain that, if Handel had written operas after the model of *Iphigénie en Tauride,* any one of them would have pleased a modern audience? For one thing, such orchestration, as circumstances would have allowed him to supply, would still be inadequate for modern demands. This is not to say that some of the operas might not possibly be revived, even as they stand, so as to command admiration, and give some pleasure. It might be so, if the audience were happily chosen. In one respect, indeed, the older form of libretto had perhaps a little advantage over those of Gluck. The interest of the main striving does not so consistently swallow up the smaller interests. It is difficult to find strong simple themes of sufficient scope to justify three hours. *Orfeo* and *Iphigénie en Aulide* seem to have a good deal of padding; and in *Iphigénie en Tauride,* a short opera, the ravings of Orestes are, strictly speaking, padding, though padding of a high interest; Iphigenia's wish to save Orestes and Pylades would have been equally strong, had they been a couple of respectable entomologists.

CHAPTER III.

Minor Criticisms.

I.

There is a little exaggeration in the statement that Handel's overtures all conform to the same pattern. The introductions range from the zero of *Israel* and the single movement of *Joshua* to the four movements of *Saul* and *Theodora,* not to reckon such things as the set of dances prefixed to *Rodrigo.* The music of the work proper is seldom anticipated, though this is found in *Deborah;* and with the rejection of this easy method, how was Handel to impart to each of the preludes a special character, seeing that the dramas themselves ran so much on the same lines ? A slight anticipatory flavour may perhaps occasionally be discerned, for example in *Athaliah, Samson, Belshazzar, Acis, Atalanta;* something, at least, in harmony with distinctive features in the works. But they who demand something characteristic of the action, or atmosphere, without anticipation of the music of the drama, are demanding an ideal probably never realised throughout a large number of works. The overture to the *Magic Flute* is excellent, but if we disregard the alleged references to freemasonry therein, there appears no reason why it should not have served as a prelude for any fairly serious drama. Had Handel addressed himself to the task of producing something distinctive for each work, and succeeded, it would have been a marvellous feat. He did not make the attempt. The method of Lully was ready to hand with its stately slow movement and fugal allegro. He took it, as Beethoven took the symphony form from his predecessors. This was not dictated by convention, for the usual Italian overture began with a quick movement. And there were overtures, which omitted the fugue, as, for instance, Bononcini's *Griselda*. Having adopted this, to our minds, severe scheme for his operas, Handel could scarcely make his oratorio overtures the more frivolous, and in fact they are framed very much on the operatic lines. Though many individual movements have great merit—perhaps the overture to *Semele* may be singled out as specially worthy of attention—these overtures do not, as a whole, rank among Handel's most important creative work.

Sir Hubert Parry ('Grove's Dictionary,' s.v. Modulation) criticises Handel's modulations, and Mr. Fuller-Maitland (*Oxf. Hist.*, iv, 99) finds him sadly to seek in 'germ' treatment. I do not gather that in either case any mental deficiency is alleged; that Handel would have had any difficulty in managing any course of modulations, that seemed to him desirable, or in treating a germ as pertinaciously as Bononcini, whose 'Per la gloria' is contrasted with 'Sweet rose and lily' in Handel's *Theodora*. Nor do I think it is suggested that there are any set rules for modulation and balance of keys, or any prescribed mode of writing arias, of which Handel was in ignorance; indeed, had there been such rules, some great composer of bygone generations would probably have betrayed them. It must be that Sir Hubert Parry has noticed how particular choruses might have been improved, and that Mr. Fuller-Maitland has discovered a better treatment of 'Angels ever bright and fair.' With such things there can be no quarrel; they take their place with Savage Landor's opinion that the fourth and fifth lines of Milton's *Paradise Lost* are 'incumbrances and deadeners of the harmony,' an opinion to which he was, of course, fully entitled. They merely illustrate those varieties of taste, without which the world would be so insipid.

In face of the rather frequent complaint, that Handel's style is very like that of Purcell, Corelli, and others, one can only remark that his is no isolated case. How like Gluck and Haydn and many another is Mozart! What a strong similarity between Wagner and Weber! But Bach, it may be said, Bach was always like himself, and like nobody else. I cannot see how this may be. We find that some twenty concertos, which once passed un-questioned as Bach's works, are mere transcriptions by him of works by Vivaldi, Telemann, and many others. One of his fugues has been restored to Eberlin. Quite a long string of works in the Bach Gesellschaft edition is marked ' of doubtful authenticity '; one of these has proved to be the work of Purcell. There is grave doubt about the authenticity of the favourite cantata *Schlage doch.* Lately Dr. Walker pointed out the strong affinity between Keiser and some part of Bach's work.* The fact is, of his local predecessors and contemporaries we know very little in England. It may be that the bulk of Bach's work stands out more markedly from its surroundings than in Handel's case; but that again may be due merely to his leaning towards elaboration and complexity, a taste which his contemporaries did not share.

Handel indulged in the practice of adapting old com-positions for new circumstances, as most composers have done, more or less, Bach and Gluck being prominent in this connexion. One of Bach's cantatas, *Steigt freudig in die Luft,* had a varied experience; first it celebrated the birthday of a grand dame, the wife of Prince Leopold of Cöthen; secondly, it served the same purpose for a 'master' (perhaps Gesner); thirdly, it emerged as a church cantata; fourthly, and lastly (so far as Spitta has traced), it honoured the birthday of J. F. Rivinus. Bach's Christmas Oratorio is a patchwork for the larger part, while some of his smaller masses are mere adaptations. Nor was any attention whatever paid to the distinction between sacred and

* 'Grove's Dictionary,' s. v. Oratorio.

secular, a feature noted by Mr. Sedley Taylor. The palmary instance, perhaps, is the transference of the song in which Pleasure incites the infant Hercules to a life of vice [in a *dramma per musica*] to the Christmas Oratorio, where it reappears, practically unchanged, as a slumber aria. As these things are fully detailed by Spitta, it is possible that they will some day be thought worthy of a place in musical histories, side by side with Handel's transferences.

From this ease of translation from sacred to secular we should probably be wrong in drawing any inference as to religious feeling in the case of either composer. ' Custom is king of all.' Handel transferred a song, with the words and music almost unaltered, from Agrippina to Mary Magdalen. Yet the Roman cardinals can scarcely have been shocked. The libretto of *Agrippina* was apparently written by Cardinal Grimani, and he was residing at Rome when *La Resurrezione* was produced.*

II.

Handel has been taxed with courting popularity, while Bach wrote rather for a select audience of two—himself and Art. If this distinction could be shown to rest on facts, an interesting question would arise, as to which was the greater benefactor of his species. However, we find a German writer† recently developing the diverging thesis, that Bach's life at Leipsic was one continuous struggle for recognition, in which he was at last content to accept

---

* Abbé, *Dictionnaire des Cardinaux*, s. v. Albani. The same authority tells of the miserable death of this Cardinal Grimani on September 19, 1710. He was Austrian Viceroy at Naples, and ruled so severely as to displease both the Pope and Saint Janvier. The Cardinal went in May to see the miracle of Saint Janvier, but the manifestation of the Saint's displeasure was so striking, that the Cardinal fell into a melancholy, and died on St. Janvier's (or St. Januarius') day in great torture.

† Herr B. F. Richter. *Bach Jahrbuch*, 1905.

defeat, composing very little in his later years. There is much to be said for this view. We certainly know that the first part of the B minor *Mass* was written in order to get a *Praedicate* from the King of Poland, and that Bach professed his readiness to devote himself to the service of this king, who, by the bye, was a Roman Catholic. Spitta considered that on his inauguration at Leipsic Bach withdrew the cantata originally intended for performance, and substituted something of a more popular character. There are quite a number of 'occasional' pieces extant, which Bach really cannot have written to please hjmself, nor yet to further the cause of Art. And as for those chorales, if they were not intended to please the people, whom were they intended to please? In truth, there seems no particular mystery in the matter. Bach was willing, it would appear, to please the people, like any other good-natured man, but for the position of public entertainer he was constitutionally ill-fitted. Spitta delivers the opinion that he would not have succeeded in opera. * Bach exhibited no contempt for those who possessed the arts of popularity; on the contrary, he was fond of going to hear the operas at Dresden, and he recommended one of his sons to devote himself to the light 'galant' style of music. The little we know of him, if it does not compel, at least admits the belief, that in his judgments he was no Gottsched, no Dennis, but leaned rather to the Patroclean gentleness and wisdom of a Sainte-Beuve. 'Beyond the mountains there are also men.' I perceive no reason why he should not have written drawing-room ballads, had he lived at the present day, and felt his powers equal to the by no means easy task of producing a really good one. He is credited with quite a number of chorales, a form of art demanding less elaboration than the ballad, and numbering among its

* ii, 624.

successful cultivators many men whose technical accomplishments were extremely slight.*

Neither was aloofness the note of Handel. He would recognise that in all *genres* of music great artistic merit may be exhibited, and he probably thought a first-rate march or minuet better than a fugue below the highest standard. This does not imply that he made the prevailing fashion his first study; else would he have become the disciple of Bononcini and Porpora. What he wrote made good its appeal to the brightest intellects of his age, to men capable of liking the fugue in *Floridante* less, because the subject did not admit of a counter-subject. Arbuthnot, Fielding, and Smollett steadfastly voiced his praise, just as in later days we find among his admirers Lord Tennyson, W. E. H. Lecky, Walter Pater, and that particularly enthusiastic Handelian, FitzGerald, the adapter of Omar Khayyám. If Handel's appeal is universal, like that of Shakespeare and Raphael, palliation is out of place. If the judgment of Spitta be sound, that ' He (Handel) succeeded, as no other of our great masters have ever done, in setting in vibration those cords of the human heart, which are independent alike of nationality and form, and are more or less the same all over the world,'† this places him on a pedestal apart, but does not diminish by one jot his claims to the highest artistic rank.

Whether contempt for the people, demophobia, be a merit rather than a disease, is a vexed question. 'Alas! not by me,' wrote Brahms of Strauss' ' Blue Danube ' waltz. And is he to be dubbed insincere? Was there insincerity behind Wagner's praise of Bellini? Rather ingratitude, black ingratitude cowers behind this deprecia-

---

* Some of the most popular of these chorales were originally secular songs. I confess I do not understand why a ' folk-song,' perhaps the effusion of some idle apprentice, ranks *necessarily* higher than, say, *The Distant Shore* of Sir Arthur Sullivan.

† ii, 144.

tion of 'popular' compositions; for they have ever supplied the sinews of war for the less popular. In England have not Bach and others climbed to performance on the broad shoulders of Handel and Mendelssohn? After all, to be popular is to be one of a 'small transfigured' band; while the unpopular are the miscellaneous mob, the proletariat.

This disparagement of 'the people' reveals itself in the pages of Sir John Hawkins, who divides Handel's compositions into such as were written for the vulgar, and those fitted for the judicious. Those written for the vulgar included such things as 'See the conqu'ring hero comes.' Mainwaring, Handel's biographer, shows signs of the same attitude, which, no doubt, was prevalent in exalted circles in those days. Human nature varies little with the lapse of centuries. There is also a hint in these writers that Handel, to a certain extent, wrote for money—like Shakespeare, I suppose, or like Sir Walter Scott. Now it is true that Handel, who was economical and unmarried, left twenty thousand pounds, the bulk of which was bequeathed to his niece, while Bach's wife was left with insufficient support, and died after all in an almshouse. But let it be remembered, not only that Handel distributed large sums in charity, but also that £20,000 was merely what a man enjoying Handel's official emoluments, and doing constant service as a conductor, might have expected to save, if he had never appealed to the public as a composer at all. This writing for money, in which he obstinately persisted, twice reduced him to bankruptcy. Is there any case known of a man's losing as much as Handel through putting his compositions before the public? Let us look at the matter from a practical standpoint. A kapellmeister to a prince, or a cantor to a city might have his *Passions* or cantatas performed by the ordinary vocalists or instrumentalists, without any considerations of pecuniary success. But where an opera or an oratorio of the later type was concerned, the pay-box had to be borne in mind.

'He who lives to please, must please to live' is the maxim graven deep on the heart of every *entrepreneur*. Generally speaking, the composer of an opera got a mere trifle for his work, and probably Handel's remuneration for operas up to 1729, at least, was comparatively modest, as he took no pecuniary risks. But when a man undertakes the management, and has to pay fifty guineas a night for the use of a theatre, to say nothing of the salaries of the performers, and when his income from other sources is no more than £600 a year, it is clear that half-filled houses will speedily bring him to ruin. He must, as a practical man, consider his audience; if it was a question of offering a minuet in the style of Bach, or a minuet like that in *Don Giovanni* —let us suppose, for argument's sake, that the musical merits were equal—the composer, as a man of sense, would prefer to bring forward the Mozartian minuet. There would be grumbling, perhaps, from those critics, who could only find pleasure in what appealed to the few, and who would not reflect that, if Handel wrote only to please *them*, he would speedily be without the power of contributing even to *their* entertainment. With a reserve income of £400 a year, one can only lose £100 a night for four nights. In the interests of music, then, in the interests of high art, Handel was obliged to include elements which should have an universal appeal; and, in the opinion of most people, he solved the problem pretty satisfactorily.

That Bach wrote for money, I shall not affirm. But I have not found any evidence that he disdained it. We hear of his occasionally accepting money or presents; we never hear, I think, of his rejecting them. It was Forkel, if I remember rightly, who thought Bach might have earned large sums, by making tours to exhibit his skill on the organ. It might have been so; and yet, from what quarter was the money to come? There were few organs except in churches, and the number of princes, who would be

likely to give presents, was limited. Bach might have left
his wife and family for a year, if the Leipzigers gave
permission, and in the end returned home, poorer in actual
cash, if with a few snuff-boxes in his portmanteaus. The
common conception, I may add, of Bach as living con-
tentedly all his days, buried in a little German town, will
really not do. He held one of the best positions in
Germany; Kuhnau had preceded him, and Telemann was
once on the point of taking the post. Nor was Bach
content to remain there; he made an attempt to obtain
a more agreeable post at Dantzic, a town then forming no
part of Germany.

Fortunately it is unnecessary to defend Handel's general
character. He was, as we know, not ascetic in the matter
of eating and drinking; few composers have been. J. S.
Bach was far from denying himself sensuous pleasures.
There is a pathetic complaint in one of his letters (Nov.
2nd, 1748), when a cask of wine, sent to him as a present,
had leaked; '. . . . it is a pity that of so noble a gift of
God the smallest drop should have been wasted' (Spitta,
iii, 272).

III.

Aesthetic discussion has been avoided here, as far as
possible. Yet there may be no harm in observing that
Handel's works, like those of any other artist, should not
be approached in the spirit of Thackeray's imagined
reviewer: 'Lady Smigsmag's new novel is amusing, but
lamentably deficient in geological information.' When
Handel wrote, 'See, the conqu'ring hero comes,' he had
no visions of ethereal beauty before him. Such lines as:

Hear I not
The Aeolian music of her sea-green plumes
Winnowing the crimson dawn?

might evoke strains of surpassing loveliness, but the approach they would celebrate would be of a very different nature from the return of the warrior Othniel. There are many things in Handel excellent in their own way, but not at all excellent in ways that are not their own. It should not need pointing out that, regarded as a love-duet, ' Go baffled coward, go' in *Samson* cannot succeed. But it is also true that as a duet between Figaro and Count Almaviva, between Florestan and Pizarro, between Loge and Alberich, it would also be a failure. It becomes a success, if success it be, because it is, in fact, a duet between the two Old Testament giants, Samson and Harapha. The great ' Torments, alas !' in the same oratorio—which I take to be the unnamed song which Mendelssohn in a letter judged as fine as any air of Handel's; it was omitted in the concert version known to him—would stand in alien majesty aloof from Lohengrin or Walther of the Preislied; it would clash as a representation of the tortures of the Christian soul, such as Bach might have depicted; but as the song of the eyeless giant Samson it cannot be gainsaid. Remarks like the above, to be sure, are the veriest commonplaces of criticism; and yet these commonplaces are so often forgotten, when the business of appreciation is actually approached. We condemn a song of Schubert's because it has not the merits peculiar to Brahms (or vice-versa); we are discontented because Achilles does not talk like Socrates, or Falstaff like Hamlet. And all the while there is room for hundreds of varieties of merit perfectly distinct and yet not necessarily unequal.

In assessing an artist's value we may look to the merits of his best or to the demerits of his worst work. Here is something to the point: 'The fame of a profuse and unequal and unresting writer has of necessity to wait longer than that of one who, like Dante Gabriel Rossetti, winnows his work and saves only that which possesses the utmost intensity and perfection, and who is thus his own anthologist. Yet the ultimate garland of the more spendthrift singer may prove to be not less in quantity, as it will certainly not rank lower in beauty of its own noble order.'* Without attempting any judgment let us observe, as an interesting fact in connexion with Handel's second and succeeding sets of 'leçons' or suites, which have not infrequently encountered severe criticism, that they were written mostly in his early years, for the purposes of practice, and that their publication in his lifetime was due to piracy.

Mr. Fuller-Maitland, who is quite justified in his conjecture that *Oriana* (1717) and *Zenobia* (1721), produced at Hamburg, may have been versions of other operas—Oriana being in fact the heroine of *Amadigi* (1715) and Zenobia of *Radamisto* (1720)—seems to consider the operasongs of Handel, with a very few exceptions, practically worthless.† Dr. Walker rates them on the whole higher than the oratorio airs.‡ In his *Ecclesiastical Polity* Richard Hooker, discussing the antagonistic heresies of Eutyches and Nestorius, utters the exhortation to 'keep warily a middle course.' May we not here keep warily a middle course, and pronounce both operas and oratorios remarkably rich in fine arias?

It may be that this and many similar differences of opinion have their fount in that versatility and universality,

* Oliver Elton. *Modern Studies*, p. 227.

† *Oxf. Hist.*, iv, 204.

‡ *History of Music in England*, p. 191. Dr. Walker, beneath the gaberdine, which perforce must cover all serious critics, is equally brilliant and equally interesting, whether the voice be Trinculo's or the voice of Trinculo's bedfellow. It is pleasant to find the garland given to 'Joys before our eyes appearing' (*Athaliah*); and not really unpleasant to find 'Honour and arms' styled 'perfunctory' and 'The Lord is a man of war' 'conventional,' for we feel that he must be using each adjective in some delightfully unconventional sense, which excites, and yet baffles, perhaps for ever, our curiosity.

which Spitta credits to Handel beyond the reach of Bach. Broad sympathy in the creator is a summons to a sympathy no less broad in the appreciator. Perhaps in criticism in the whole sphere of art too little importance is attached to range and variety of thought, when estimating the achievements of an artist. We are apt to pay too much attention to his value to *us,* rather than to his absolute value 'sub specie aeternitatis.' I confess to a certain sympathy with Mattheson, who compares his own achievements with those of Handel: he had done a vast amount of good work in writing and theorising, which should not be overlooked in comparing their total respective worths. As a man, as a producer or 'maker' in the widest sense, he might possibly establish his claim to something like equality, though for *us* his value is now small. Suppose A devotes himself to one sphere of thought, and reaches heights which no successor ever scales in that particular region, is he therefore greater than B, who cultivates a dozen fields, and finds in each a successor who does still better work? Having now 'Adelaide' and Walther's 'Preislied,' to us the relative value of 'Where'er you walk' (*Semele*), 'Love in her eyes' (*Acis*), or 'Ye verdant hills' (*Susanna*) may (conceivably) be a shade lower; where more modern composers join hands with him they may equal or surpass, using at least a newer garb, the kindred feelings in Handel's scores. It is possible that the airs (almost successive) 'Verdi prati,' 'Ombre pallide,' 'Credete al mio dolore,' 'Un momento di contento,' 'Sta nell' Ircana,' in *Alcina*—to take an example—may have been surpassed, each in its several way, by different later composers. None the less any man who can sit down lightly to match the set is very cordially to be congratulated. Handel, in truth, 'warmed both hands at the fire of life.' Gervinus has elaborated a parallel between him and Shakespeare, and

Gervinus started with this initial advantage, that he had a fair knowledge of the works of both artists. Call Handel a Shakespeare a little stiff in the joints, call him a Shakespeare in buckram, establish what distinction you will between the heights of the two achievements, still a resemblance more or less marked may be argued for, one would fancy, with as much ease and quiet comfort as any rival similitude.

CHAPTER IV.

Foreign .Material.

I.

'I DID it,' said St. Augustine, 'compelled by no hunger, nor poverty, but through a cloyedness of well-doing, and a pamperedness of iniquity. For I stole that of which I had enough and much better.' Handel's 'known wealth,' like Dryden's, was great. To the proofs of his wide-branching renown, given in Chapter I., we may here add that in Leipsic itself his fame exceeded that of J. S. Bach, as Mr. Balfour has noted in his brilliant and stimulating essay.* To Klopstock it was an abiding consolation that Handel the German counterbalanced the English superiority in literature. To his middle operas a writer at Paris (1734, or earlier) gave the preference over all contemporary compositions :

'Flavius, Tamerlan, Othon, Renaud, Cæsar,
Admete, Siroé, Rodelinde, et Richard,
Eternels monumens dressés à sa mémoire,
Des Opera Romains surpasserent la gloire.
Venise lui peut-elle opposer un rival ?'†

What are we to make then of that saying imputed by Wesley to Salomon, that Handel's English reputation 'was wholly constituted on the spoils of the continent'? This Salomon, well-known in connexion with Haydn's symphonies, was born at Bonn (1745), spent his youth at Bonn, a spot not especially remarkable then as a musical centre,

---

* The Right Hon. A. J. Balfour, M.P. *Essays and Addresses.*

† As quoted in Chrysander, ii, 184. This preference of Handel to Bononcini, who is himself placed above Alessandro Scarlatti, is the more noteworthy, in that Bononcini visited Paris from time to time to give concerts.

made a concert tour as a violinist in 1765, was concert-
meister at Rheinsberg, and made a short stay at Paris
before reaching London in 1781. We may picture him,
if we will, as consuming his leisure hours in rummaging
among ancient and still-forgotten manuscripts, and remembering their contents so well as to recognise their strains
on becoming acquainted with Handel's works in England.
But a far simpler explanation will suggest that Salomon or
Wesley was a little autocratic in the use of language.
Everyone, in truth, knows that the bulk of these borrowings of themselves attest Handel's originality with a force
absolutely irresistible. He erects a towering monument to
the wisdom of Goethe's opinion (Sprüche, 5th section),
that the fruitful expansion or transformation of a borrowed
thought is the finest mark of originality (das schönste
Zeichen der Originalität).

Undoubtedly Handel made use of the music of other
composers; this fact emerges, after we have cleared away a
number of blundering accretions. Some of the smaller
alleged borrowings crumble up under examination; and
even should anyone not be entirely convinced of the Handelian authorship of the works attributed to Erba, Urio, and
Stradella, he will recognise that no one can be expected to
take account of broken-backed possibilities. For practical
purposes we have to deal with borrowings from a number
of composers, among whom, after sifting, the prominent
names are found to be those of Graun, Muffat, Clari,
Habermann, Keiser and Kerl; and we are to consider
whether Handel dealt quite openly, or whether on the
contrary he worked like some Locusta, brewing deadly
potions in the shades of night, with fear and trembling.

If this question could but be settled by 'common sense,'
contentment would reign. Unfortunately 'common sense'
is a steed far too amenable to the bit. He stands equally
at the service of Bigendians and Littleendians, Shakespear-
ians and Baconians, Homoousians and Homoiousians.

Perhaps recognising this, Mr. Sedley Taylor* has betaken himself rather to a study of the history of the time, and has, though with a little hesitation, favoured conclusions which may be summarised as follows:

1. Plagiarism was accounted a serious offence in those days, as is proved by the well-known case of Bononcini.

2. No traces of acknowledgment can be found in Handel's scores, nor yet in his note-books which are found to contain extracts from other composers.

3. His contemporaries, and also the historians Hawkins and Burney, who wrote some years after Handel's death, are quite silent on the subject; indeed Hawkins at least makes a point of emphasising Handel's originality.

4. Had Handel's borrowings—some of them verging on the procedure of Bononcini—been known in his lifetime, an uproar would have been raised by his enemies; yet of this there is not the slightest trace.

I think this will be recognised as a fair summary of the reasons which have led Mr. Taylor and others to regard the transactions as secret. I could wish that the exact features of the secrecy had been limned with greater precision. It cannot mean surely that the quotations were not conspicuously advertised to all and sundry, to the general public. To those frequent adaptations from Homer and other poets Lord Tennyson drew no public attention, I believe; and when an American offered incense at Freshwater, I doubt whether the late laureate always introduced the blind old Greek. A few readers recognise a number of the references; exceptional scholars may recognise nearly all; but the mass of readers are steeped in an unconsciousness only exceeded by their serene indifference. A host of the readers of Wordsworth cannot make out why he emphasises some of his finest lines by inverted commas; and when they meet the words:

* *The indebtedness of Handel to other composers.* Pitt Press.

> " ' There is a pleasure in poetic pains
> Which only poets know.' 'Twas rightly said "

the good taste of this self-laudation strikes them as very questionable. Or. take those ' Ungarische Tänze ' of Brahms. The mass of hearers or buyers do not know, the editions do not tell them, that the melodies are not original.

By secrecy something more must be meant than this kind of reserve, which keeps enlightenment for the few. Can it be meant that Handel issued the revelations merely to the inner circle of his admirers? But such secrets could never be kept; the friend of to-day is the foe of to-morrow, as Handel had found in 1733; to reveal them at all would imply that he had no objection to the secrets being known to everybody. If we think out the position, the charge must mean that Handel confided in none, save perhaps his amanuensis Smith, or the owner of some particular manuscript, exacting solemn vows of secrecy, and taking great care, moreover, that his manuscripts or copies should remain under lock and key, secure from casual intruders into his rooms. I shall assume, at any rate, that this is the course of conduct imputed; otherwise the discussion would become ineffably frivolous. It is as constituting an attempt to prove this course of conduct that the arguments of Mr. Taylor will be subjected to examination. Afterwards reasons will be given for thinking such a course extremely improbable, if not absolutely impossible. It is unfortunate that thoroughness cannot be combined with brevity; and I offer this lengthy discussion solely for the reason which decided Charles Lamb's raven to go to the wedding in a black suit—it was the only one he had. The breaking of eggs precedes the making of omelettes, and historical study is often the sole avenue to historical truth.

II.

No harm will be done, but rather a better general estimate of the argument will be attained, if we observe first, how easily it might be made to apply to other composers; and this may be done without the suggestion of any other parallelism than what concerns the argument alone. The same reasoning may establish equally the mortality of Tom Thumb and Giant Blunderbore; nor will differences of inches affect the parallelism. Let us turn first to J. S Bach.

(1) Though many of Bach's autographs have perished, yet on those that remain, and equally on contemporary copies, it might be difficult to discover a single real trace of acknowledgment. Yet some twenty concertos once supposed to be original works of Bach have proved to be mere adaptations of concertos by Vivaldi, Telemann, Marcello, Duke Ernest of Saxe-Weimar, and other composers at present unidentified. Now if Bach's originals ever contained these acknowledgments, why were they not transcribed by the copyists? It is true that on one copy made at Leipsic in 1739 twelve of these are styled adaptations from Vivaldi; but as the greater part are certainly not by that Italian composer, the information could not have been derived from the original MSS., nor yet from J. S. Bach himself. It need only represent an independent discovery made at some period by the owner of the MS., who had become acquainted with some of Vivaldi's concertos. In another case, where a copy notes the use of a theme by Legrenzi, Griepenkerl who saw the now-lost original, reported that Legrenzi's name was not there mentioned. No trace of acknowledgment of the use of Handel's *Almira*. No trace on the original MS. of the cantata containing a five-part aria transcribed absolutely verbatim from Rosenmüller. One might draw up quite a formidable list of composers from whom Bach is believed

to have derived themes.* (2) His biographers were a
son and a pupil, yet neither they nor any contemporary
mentions these things. (3) The case of Bononcini would
not be unknown in Germany. (4) Bach had many enemies.
One of them, Scheibe, printed a criticism in 1737, yet
overlooked this splendid chance of attacking Bach's
originality, of representing him as a mere mangler of the
ideas of men greater than himself, for so would have run
the contemporary verdict as to relative capacity.

Here then is apparently a case against Bach, which is,
I have no doubt, error-begetting, and yet is not so easy
to meet as might be thought. Mattheson mentions Bach
as being particularly successful in treating given themes
(on the organ), but that might only refer to extempore
playing, not to works fully written out. In another passage
Mattheson seems to be referring to Bach (though his name
is not mentioned), when he quotes a rather inferior version
of the long theme and counterpoint of the great G minor
organ fugue, and adds that he knows well the inventor,
and who formerly had worked it out with great skill.
One would incline to think that Mattheson intended a
distinction between the original inventor and the skilful
treater; however, Spitta and other biographers will have
it that Bach must be meant in each case.† We seem then
to be without any certain contemporary references. And
suppose it argued that Bach's transcriptions were made at
Weimar, while the young Duke was living there, or had
recently died, so that secrecy was impossible, the answer
is obvious. It is only conjecture that these works were
written at Weimar; and even if they were originally written

---

* See Spitta's biography and *L'Esthétique de Jean-Sébastien Bach*, by
Monsieur A. Pirro.

† I fail to see the slightest ground for Spitta's suggestion that this
suppression of Bach's name indicates hostility on the part of Mattheson.
It was Mattheson's constant custom to suppress names; and such a method
of showing enmity would have been childish or fatuous. An enemy would
have made no reference whatever to the subject.

there, how would that prevent Bach passing them off as his own in the eyes of the Leipzigers? Besides Bach has also adapted—though more freely, especially in the fugues —some sonatas from Reinken's *Hortus Musicus;* again these were long supposed original works of Bach, and Reinken, let it be noted, lived at Hamburg, far from Leipsic. It might be said of the use of the five-part aria of Rosenmüller, that he was a deceased Leipsic worthy, and that in adopting his composition in place of the usual chorale Bach wished to do honour to his predecessor.* Then why did he not advertise the fact on his MS.? And why, when doing a similar thing by a four-part aria of Vetter (also a deceased Leipsic musician), did he introduce a few alterations?

A stubborn attitude of suspicion cannot easily be changed by such arguments as readily come to hand. Besides, there are other perturbing circumstances. In a cantata without author's name but catalogued as J. S. Bach's, and certainly containing one movement by him, is a whole movement attributed elsewhere to Telemann, besides another movement which Spitta judges to have a Telemann groundwork, with alterations by Bach.† If the catalogue is right we are enabled to view Bach as passing off as his own what contained a whole movement by Telemann. Or again, there is extant without author's name a mass in C minor in Bach's handwriting, which, says Spitta, is on the one hand certainly not Bach's yet on the other hand certainly contains one duet written by him.‡ Now this mass was advertised as Bach's after his death. I cannot help suspecting that Bach occasionally put together cantatas with music from different sources, without troubling to indicate those sources on his MSS.; and if such

* Spitta. The Bach Gesellschaft editors suggest lack of time as Bach's reason.

† Spitta, ii, 716.

‡ Spitta, iii, 29.

an hypothesis be not ruled out as inadmissible, I would suggest that the doubt as to the authorship of the motet 'Ich lasse dich nicht' ('I wrestle and pray') would be explained by the supposition that Bach worked over a composition of his uncle, J. C. Bach, so that after his death, if not in his lifetime, it passed as his own. However, it will be agreed, whatever view we take of particular cases, that the men of those days were remarkably indifferent as to nice assignments of authorship.

As to Beethoven and his alleged use of folk-songs, to say nothing of occasional themes from Mozart and Haydn (unacknowledged), let us remember that Weber was accused of plagiarism when he introduced folk-songs into *Der Freischütz* (1821);* that Beethoven had critics and opponents; and that Schindler, Wegeler, and Ries seem to tell us nothing, except that Schindler says a small fragment in the *Pastoral Symphony* is a phrase of Austrian national melody—an observation he may have made for himself. How could it happen that Schindler, who lived long in close intercourse with Beethoven, has nothing to say about the far more interesting and important borrowings in the *Pastoral Symphony* alone? From the point of view of gain to a reputation for originality and variety, it is arguable that these are more important than any borrowing of Handel. Once again let it be observed that reasoning concerns itself not at all with size. It is:

'As full, as perfect, in a hair as heart.'

* R. A. Streatfield. *The Opera*, p. 92.

CHAPTER V.

A MEDLEY OF PARALLELS.

I.

LET us turn to the case of Bononcini. What really was the offence alleged against this composer? That he had openly introduced, though without MS. acknowledgment, a movement by another composer into a work of his own? Nothing of the kind. The charge ran that he had presented to the Academy of Antient Musick, about the year 1727, as a specimen of his own composition, a madrigal which in every respect was identical with a madrigal of Lotti's published in 1705. But that was only the beginning. When the fact was pointed out to him, he asserted his own authorship, and deliberately and persistently, nay really valiantly, taxed Lotti with plagiarism. 'It was thought,' says Hawkins, 'a very dishonest thing in him to assume, and that in terms so positive and express, the merit of a composition which he could not but know was the work of another.' Observe the heightening of the offence in the addition 'terms so positive and express.' With the truth of the charge against Bononcini we are not concerned, but we cannot acquit both him and Lotti; it is one or the other. No suggestion of defective memory will serve, for both were precise and circumstantial as to the origin of the composition.

Now a world that thoroughly disapproved of shameless lying might yet not have the slightest objection to Handel's openly adapting, say, an organ-canzona of Kerl's, nor think the fact a jewel worthy of a prominent place on the stretched forefinger of time. Only if we have already assumed secrecy on the part of Handel, can the Bononcini case have any relevance; and then how superfluous it becomes! No need of parallels to prove the impropriety of what would not bear the light.

Yet let us guard ourselves against concluding the England of those days peculiarly sensitive on such points. 'At Venice and at Vienna all is calm,' remarks Lotti playfully, and the same may be suspected of England outside the sphere of the Academy. If Bononcini was 'hounded out,' then is 'hounding out' a very leisurely and dignified procedure. Do but observe the dates. The Academy writes to Lotti first in February, 1731. The correspondence continues for months, and is finally published towards the beginning of 1732. Had the Londoners been in a state of tension all this time, merely curbing in their righteous anger through fear of a miscarriage of justice, the pent-up storm should have hurried Bononcini out of England in less than a week. Yet, when its fury burst, was he a penny the worse? On June 24th, 1732, Handel's *Acis* was succeeded at the same theatre by a cantata produced 'by command of the Queen and in presence of the Royal Family.' Of this cantata the composer was Bononcini, and we are not told of any riot or uproar when he conducted the performance. He still lived in London. In 1733 his *Griselda* was revived; in 1734 his *Astarto*. When he left England is not certainly known with exactness, but it was apparently some time in 1733. And there is nothing to prevent our ascribing his departure to quite ordinary reasons. His later operas had failed; they were considered far inferior to his earlier inspirations, such as *Griselda* and *Astarto*. Moreover, they were composed, like Handel's, largely in the earlier or Scarlattian style. Now when Senesino and the nobility quarrelled with Handel in the spring of 1733, they needed, to oppose the Saxon, something more attractive than the played-out Bononcini. They very wisely preferred to invite Porpora with the prestige of novelty both in style and personality. Here probably is to be found the main reason why Bonon-

cini found 'his occupation gone.' Doubtless the 'Academy'
affair would provide a pretext for some patrons, already
aweary of the Italian, to withdraw their support, but the
general public would care little for this trumpery squabble,
as they would regard it, between Bononcini and the
'Academics.' And such of the inner circle as were generally favourable to him, would incline rather to criticise the
officious, if not malicious, pertinacity of his opponents.
Nowadays when hands are laid on a materialised spirit, and
the fair medium meets the astonished gaze, her admirers
seem to be chiefly indignant at the disgustingly ungentle-
manly conduct of the marplot. In 1732, we note, ' Hurlo-
thrumbo ' Johnson was not ashamed to associate himself
with Bononcini as not receiving proper support in England;
time would repair the neglect. In 1734 the writer of a
humorous defence of Handel (Arbuthnot ?) pokes a little
fun at Bononcini's mild heroine Griselda, but of the
madrigal he says not one syllable.

Indeed, Lotti himself in his letters seems to regard it
as a paltry absurd business; Bononcini could at any time
have written a madrigal as good or better; and this view
receives support from Burney (*Hist.*, iv, 323) : ' The
counterpoint of this madrigal is certainly correct, but it is
dry, and all the subjects of fugue are such as had been
used by thousands before Lotti was born.'

II.

The above quotation from Burney has its elements of
surprise, if we put on it the interpretation which is natural
though perhaps not quite certain. If the fugue themes
were not original, Lotti *was* a plagiarist after a sort.
And as Mr. Sedley Taylor insists (p. 176), plagiarism
was regarded as a serious offence, and what no man who
had a ' regard for his fame and reputation ' could afford
to leave unrebutted. This plagiarism is, in truth, a procedure at once unanimously discountenanced and universally practised. Almost all great artists have been plagiar-

ists. Dean Swift, it is true, boasted that he had never taken a hint, but against this let us set the remark of Warburton : 'Dryden, I observe, borrows from want of leisure, Pope from want of genius; Milton out of pride, and Addison out of modesty.' How elastic or how indefinable is the term ! Dr. Croft in his 'Burial Service' (1724) retained part of the setting by Purcell 'for reasons,' remarks he in his preface, 'which will be obvious to every artist.'* Ah ! but this is not plagiarism, it might be argued, for he openly acknowledges the debt. Suppose, however, that seeing the reasons *were* so obvious, he had omitted, in the serenity of innocence, to mention the fact, would there then have been plagiarism ? Make acknowledgment your test, and Brahms will remain of unflawed virtue in one instance, a phrase of Domenico Scarlatti which he acknowledged, but a shameless plagiarist in a sheaf of other cases. Did Mendelssohn approach the forbidden thing, because the quartet in *Elijah* 'Cast thy burden' is an arrangement of a chorale ? The fact is not mentioned in the ordinary editions. When Dr. Johnson inserted nine lines in the *Traveller,* did Goldsmith, who printed them without acknowledgment, commit a plagiarism ? I am afraid the general public was deceived. But the questions would be endless; the subject swells to such a size as to evade the grasp. Nor are we much helped by a reference to the 'custom of the times.' Such a thing there never was. Such a thing there really never could be, having application over the whole of Europe. Try to learn the custom, and two equally competent authorities in the same town might give diametrically opposed answers. When the law courts in a commercial case consider the 'custom of the trade' of a particular town, each party to the suit marshals its array of unimpeachable witnesses, who will deliver opinions, perfectly perspicuous, but hopelessly irreconcilable. Fog envelopes the whole subject.

* Hawkins.

Yet perhaps two things may be regarded as certain. Critics of all times have been beyond measure inconsistent :

> 'That in the captain 's but a choleric word,
> Which in the soldier is flat blasphemy.'

What 'Mr. Handel condescended' to do was not, to Charles Burney, the properest thing to be allowed the small composer. And Burney in his inconsistency has the world with him. Professor Saintsbury, dealing with the borrowings of Molière, seems to regard the rights of the big man as incontestable. And assuredly to appropriate what you did not write, but at any time might have written yourself, is a different thing from appropriating what you did not compose, and never in your life could have composed. We must at least allow for this principle having weight with Handel's contemporaries. The second position not likely to be contested is this, that intentional and deliberate secrecy is all the world over quite indefensible.

Of the literary borrowings of that age some idea may be gleaned from the account of Parnell in Johnson's *Lives of the Poets*. And from what we read in Burney and elsewhere, it would seem that the librettists in England, such as Haym or Rolli seldom took the trouble to name the Italian poets whose works they were adapting, even when the alterations were extremely slight. So it was in Germany too.* Frederick the Great acted like the rest; he translated the text of Voltaire's *Mérope* for the purposes of an opera, adding lyrics himself; yet Voltaire's name is absent from the libretto. The frequency of this phenomenon makes it quite inadmissible to impute any real intention to deceive.† Such a suggestion in the case of Frederick and *Mérope* would be most grotesquely absurd; but acknowledgments were evidently regarded as unnecessary, and when they were made, it was probably because the name of the first writer was thought likely to attract. Nowadays 'from the French' is considered enough when it is thought advisable to mention the obligation at all.

* Herr Mayer Reinach, 'S.I.M.G.,' i, 470.
† *cf.* Chrysander, ii, 179.

CHAPTER VI.

ACKNOWLEDGMENT.

THIS leads us to the non-acknowledgment argument. As Mr. Sedley Taylor emphasises the fact that Handel's choruses, in which the specially criticised borrowings are mostly found, were not accessible in print during his lifetime, it would appear that no importance is attached to non-acknowledgment in print. In truth it was the publishers alone that such things concerned. These publishers printed just what they liked with or without the composer's leave, affixing or omitting his name. If an opera was the work of several writers they might only name one; *Gianguir* for instance was advertised as Hasse's, though but a small fraction was of his composition.* We may be sure that had Handel wished them to add notes, saying that this or that quotation came from this or that place (where however it might not be original) the publishers would have rebelled and struck out these' notes. Extra trouble and expense would have been entailed; it was uncustomary and it would not make the edition sell any better. Moreover, unless of portentous length, such notes might be very misleading. Are we to suggest the use of a phrase of Sir John Hawkins ' taken from ' ? Why, that might mean everything or it might mean practically nothing !

The question of MSS. and note-books is different. Here we change generations; we no longer have contemporaries in our minds. For it is clear that had Handel wished to enlighten his public, never, never, could he have

---

* Burney, *Hist.*, iv, 448. In another place 'the music [of *Dido* and *Semiramis*] was not entirely composed by Hasse, though printed under his name.'—*Hist.*, iv, 457.

chosen a more absurd advertisement sheet than a manuscript which none would see. And imagine a *posse* of
infuriated opponents bursting into 57 Brook St., indignant
that Handel had told them not a word about Clari or
Habermann, and conceive, if it be possible, their wrath
melting like snowflakes when he triumphantly produced
his note-book from an inner pocket! Really this 'non-
acknowledgment' argument implies the distinct charge,
that Handel wished to deceive posterity; with contemporaries it can have no possible concern. Nothing but confusion would result from an attempt to treat these two
charges together; of each the strength or weakness can
be examined much better apart.

Now what is presupposed by this 'posterity-deception'
charge, for that it was made with some sense of what it
means, with 'an eye on the object,' we are bound to
assume? Must we think that Handel made the attempt,
though the MSS. or printed editions were circulating in
England during his lifetime? Must we think that in
furtherance of his dark designs, he carefully left behind
him his own copies, with names and titles complete? Why
then, his plotting would break down on the very threshold!
These suppositions will be rejected with scorn. He des-
troyed, annihilated, blotted from the face of the earth
his own copies, the sole copies in England to the best of
his belief; a copy of a motet by Legrenzi (slightly used in
Samson), with a ceremonious ascription in Handel's own
writing, is to be explained as an oversight, which is, of
course, quite possible. Yet how vain were his endeavours!
That benignant fortune which had so jealously guarded
the shores of Albion, thrusting back all possible rival
copies from 1670 to 1759, so completely turned a cat in
a pan that by 1831, when Crotch wrote, hardly one of
Handel's known sources but had come within his ken!
Clari and Habermann, Graun and Muffat, Kerl, Carissimi,
Lotti, etc., not one could resist the magnetic attraction.

Keiser is absent, no doubt, but then there is no reason to imagine Handel ever had a copy of his *Octavia* in England. ' Urio ' or rather ' Uria ' is not wanting; ' Erba ' and ' Stradella ' indeed are not in the list, but they too emerged in England, and in England alone a few years later. Much old music has been examined or published on the continent since Crotch's time, yet, curiously enough (Keiser's *Octavia* excepted), without fresh finds worth noting. Is not this most marvellous? Kerl and Cesti were especially alert; just that particular duet of Cesti's, just that particular canzona of Kerl's, confront us in the pages of Sir John Hawkins (1776). Such restful torpor before 1759, such vivacious mobility afterwards, infecting, not the whole mass of foreign music, but just enough to supply what was wanted for the unmasking! I suppose those who reckon Urio (or Uria) among the creditors reject that statement on the 1781 MS. that it was copied from a MS. once possessed by Handel; and it must be admitted that MS. statements or ascriptions should be received with caution; however, there it is. Those who have no appetite for the marvellous, who think providential interpositions should not be 'multiplied beyond necessity,' and yet wish to retain the posterity-deception theory, will peruse with gratitude the pages which remove the incubus of Erba, Urio, and Stradella.* Yet even then they will ' tug the labouring oar.' How can their tale, even thus chastened, compete with the simple unobjectionable supposition, that the works were left behind by Handel, either in his own library or already in circulation? And if this simple hypothesis be accepted, how could there be any hope of deceiving posterity, and what becomes of the non-acknowledgment argument?

It will probably occur to most people that Handel could not be expected to fill up his MSS. with notes explaining

---

* For special reasons, however, the advent of a serenata bearing Stradella's name need excite no surprise; see p 161.

the exact origin and extent of all foreign material. Neither he nor Bach would be thinking of the days when his manuscripts would be closely scrutinised; else they would have acted very differently, and given us vast stores of interesting information. If they had used some brief phrase, e.g., 'taken from,' discoverers would still be very much at a loss to know what was meant, unless the originals were accessible; and then little value would attach to the information, as events have proved.

The note-books contain jottings made for practical purposes without any thought of posterity in Handel's mind. He will sometimes begin a page on lines 3—4 or 7—8, and then perhaps the music of lines 1—2, as it proceeds, must creep into all manner of corners that may be vacant. He does not bind himself to copy exactly even the fragments he extracts; words are nearly always omitted as useless; nevertheless had this been done to hoodwink posterity, he would carefully have refrained from conveying those few German words into his extracts from Graun's *Passion*. There was always a chance that an acute person would perceive their significance. In what is, I believe, the only known full copy of another composer's work by Handel—the motet of Legrenzi—the title is prefixed. Bach, on the other hand, possessed quite a number of church compositions (many copied by his own hand), which yet bore no author's name, with the consequence that a number were advertised for sale as his after his death. Handel made his jottings very hastily and could have had no object in giving himself the superfluous information that he was extracting from this or that composer. And it will be allowed, I believe, that the naming of sources in making extracts is a habit only ingrained in scholars through vigilant care, and after many an annoying experience. Let me quote the misfortune of Canon Liddon, whose transparent honesty none will question. In his University Sermons (1865) occurred passages, which a hostile critic

referred to a French source. 'The first sermon in my book,' ran Liddon's explanation, 'was composed from MS. notes, compiled or jotted down at various times, for the purpose of extempore preaching, *and unaccompanied, I regret to say, in almost all cases, by any reference to the source from which the several notes had been taken.'*
Twelve years later (in 1865) he had forgotten the sources of the extracts. To Liddon, as to Handel, the references would be quite useless for his immediate purpose; and where nothing was wanted nothing was done.

* The italics are ours. I owe this example to a newspaper article.

CHAPTER VII.

Contemporary Usage.

I.

The third item next claims our attention, the silence of contemporaries and historians like Hawkins and Burney. Before attempting to estimate this 'argument from silence,' let us look at the facts rather more closely than has been done by Mr. Sedley Taylor. Let me reproduce first of all the passage from Sir John Hawkins.*

" And here it may not be impertinent to observe, what every person conversant with his works will be inclined to believe, viz., that his style was original and self-formed; and were evidence of the fact wanting, it is capable of proof by his own testimony, for in a conversation with a very intelligent person now living, on the course of his studies, Mr. Handel declared that after he became master of the rudiments of his art, he forbore to study the works of others, and ever made it a rule to follow the suggestions of his own fancy."

What have we here ?   Merely the observation that Handel's *style* was original, the rest of the extract being ' evidence of the fact.' Now really Hawkins was quite capable of distinguishing between style and material, and we need not impute such gross obtuseness to him. Nobody will contend that the originality of Bach's style is affected by his reproductions from Rosenmüller and Vetter, or his transcriptions from Vivaldi and Reinken, or his frequent use of chorales. And if you were to read Mr. Taylor's meaning into this alleged statement by Handel, you would find with surprise that he must ingenuously have confessed

---

* *Hist.*, v, 412. Cf. Sedley Taylor, p. ix.

to systematic borrowings *before* 'he became master of the rudiments of his art.' However, there is no need to labour the point; it is sufficient to turn to Book iv, p. 92, where Sir John remarks:

"And here it may be noted that the chorus in Mr. Handel's oratorio of Samson 'Hear, Jacob's God' is taken from that in [Carissimi's] Jephtha 'Plorate filiae Israel.'"

Mr. Taylor's inference seems doubly invalid.

As Mr. Taylor himself has doubts as to the relevance of the passage he quotes from Burney, it may be left inviolate. Burney, in fact, appears to be discussing Handel's claims to be the founder of oratorio. Far more to the purpose is the passage:

"Handel is supposed to have availed himself of Clari's subjects, and sometimes more, in the choruses of Theodora." *Hist.,* iii, 536.

In another passage (*Hist.,* iii, 521) we find:

"In this work [of Turini] there is a canon, upon the subject of which Handel has composed one of his finest instrumental fugues; but, according to his usual practice, whenever he adopted another man's thoughts, he has enlivened and embellished this theme, like a man of true genius, with a counter subject, and shewn that he saw farther into its latent fertility than the original inventor."

So far from complete was Burney's ignorance! Mr. Shedlock had previously quoted these passages in an article in the 'Musical Times' (July—September, 1901). To an article of his, I think, I owe a quotation from Scheibe's Preface to *Ueber die musikalische Composition* (1773), p. 53: 'Handel and Hasse, those renowned men . . . . have—particularly the first—made frequent use of his [Keiser's] inventions, with great profit.' But they turned them, he says, into new and original thoughts. 'Mattheson and Telemann have more than once assured me of this' (Mattheson und Telemann haben mir dieses mehr als einmal bekräftiget ').

There is a passage in Burney's sketch of the Handel Commemoration, p. 55, which Mr. Sedley Taylor has very oddly overlooked. "Scheiben [*sic*] in his Criticus Musicus published at Leipzig in 1745 says: 'Handel, though he often worked upon his own material, yet disdained not to use the thoughts of others; particularly those of Reinhard Keiser.'" This, let it be noted, was introduced without the slightest necessity into a work written in Handel's honour; so that Burney could scarcely have been shocked.

When may we imagine these conversations with Mattheson and Telemann to have taken place? About 1736-40, of course, when Scheibe also was living at Hamburg; that is, in the lifetime not only of Handel but of Keiser. That Mattheson—the old friend, whose foil would have hurried Handel to an early grave, had not a button intervened—should talk about such things was only natural, for in his short life of Handel (*Ehrenpforte*, 1740) he wrote that when *Agrippina*, written at Venice, was produced at Hamburg in 1718, people observed various imitations, exactly like the originals from *Porsenna*, &c. ('verschiedene den Originalien gäntzlich ähnliche Nachahmungen aus Porsenna, &c). This *Porsenna* was an opera of Mattheson's (1702). What Mattheson's '&c.,' indicated is of course unknown, but *Agrippina* contained quotations from Keiser's *Octavia* (1705); we may therefore conclude that at least as early as 1718 Handel's use of Keiser was known at Hamburg. Yet, like Burney and Hawkins, Mattheson betrays no horror. Moreover, singularly enough, though he translated with slight additions and corrections (1761) Mainwaring's *Life of Handel* (1760), and was by no means backward in correcting Mainwaring or criticising Handel on proper occasions, he seems to have made no comment on the remarks of Mainwaring (quoted by Mr. Taylor) about Handel's grandeur of conception, which predominates in his choruses, coming purely from nature, or that 'in his fugues and overtures he is quite original.' These things are true with a perennial truth; and Mattheson was not so feather-brained as to treat his readers to petty and irrelevant cavils. He had some sense of proportion. A biographer, like any other artist, is not to 'say all he can, but only all he ought.'*

II.

To the names of Bach, Handel, and Hasse may be added the name of Corelli,† as using borrowed themes and those not confined to fugue subjects, still less to hackneyed traditional subjects, as seems to be suggested in the Oxford History, iv, 87. Are we then justified in supposing such things utterly unknown in England during Handel's lifetime? The question demands a little patience, for of direct statements there are naturally none, and we must wearily adjust our ideas by observing scattered details.

There is a theme used in *Joshua* (1747) 'Heroes when with glory burning,' which seems to be assigned by Herr Kretzschmar ‡ to an opera of Keiser's, *La forza della virtù* (1700) with the words 'Amor macht mich zum Tyrannen.' But prior to *Joshua* Handel had used the same theme in *Agrippina* (1708 ?), 'L'alma mia fra le tempeste,' and adapted it for the final chorus of *Muzio Scaevola* (1721), 'Sì sarà più dolce amore con la cara libertà.' And this very theme it is that appears in Hawkins in a duet bearing the name of Cesti (1620 ?—1669), 'Cara e dolce libertà, L'alma mia consoli tu più non vivo [?] servitù . . .'

It also appears, with the same words and almost the same music throughout, in a book of ariettas printed in England, and bearing the name of Alessandro Scarlatti (1659 ?—1725).§ Now an inspection of the music will

---

* Mainwaring's words are discussed, p. 76.

† Burney, *Hist.*, iii, 557, on the authority of a friend who had talked with Geminiani.

‡ 'S.I.M.G.,' iii, 285.

§ If we must take ascriptions seriously, I suppose this is more than a parallel to the use of Kerl's canzona by Handel. But 'the wise man lends a very academic faith' to ascriptions. The 'Scarlatti' version is quoted in part, Chrysander, i, 199.

convince anyone that the versions set down to Cesti and Scarlatti were not constructed from Handel's compositions. Yet the curious resemblance of words forbids any resort to 'accident.' We are forced then to conclude that the duet arose prior to the versions of Handel, and also prior to that of Keiser (if I understand Herr Kretzschmar's meaning aright).

Where then was *Agrippina* produced? At Venice, where Cesti died; and the theme was also used in a cantata *Ah! crudel*, written for the Marchese Ruspoli at Rome, where Cesti was born, and where (alternatively) Scarlatti was residing at the very time. We may with confidence affirm that the theme was openly used, with the intention that it should be recognised, in Italy. And with a confidence no whit less assured we may assert the same of England. For the opera *Muzio Scaevola* was the one written conjointly, and yet in a sort of rivalry, with Bononcini and Mattei (or else Ariosti), Italians who would be sure to know the melody. The similarity of words then establishes beyond cavil the intentional openness of the reference. And yet in spite of the peculiar celebrity of this opera, Sir John Hawkins prints the duet without any reference to Handel.*

In view of the continental practices and the references in Burney (which imply more than an odd case or two), the above illustration is of itself sufficient to display Handel openly doing in England what Bach did in Germany. At the cost of tediousness, however, some other illustrations will be given, as so many writers have doubted the openness of such quotations. Take the quotation from the motet of Gallus (an Austrian composer), *Ecce quomodo justus moritur*, in Handel's *Funeral Anthem*, 'But their name liveth evermore.' Now this anthem formed the

* Herr A. Schering, 'Z.I.M.G.,' ix, 7, has pointed out that Handel used at Rome in *La Resurrezione* (1708) a theme found in Corelli's Sonatas Op. 5 (1700). Corelli was living at Rome in 1708, as Herr Schering notes.

Requiem of a German lady, Queen Caroline, and a fragment of melody from a German chorale is introduced at the beginning of the anthem. Gallus' work was very well known in Germany; at Leipsic in 1721 Kuhnau introduced a portion of it into a *Passion* of his own, whether with or without 'acknowledgment,' I do not know.* And Handel did not omit to point the quotation by selecting for its introduction the approximate equivalent of the Latin words 'et erit in pace memoria ejus.'

Astorga's *Stabat Mater* was composed in London about 1710, it is believed; it was certainly well-known in England. To this *Stabat Mater* are credited the themes of 'Then shall they know' (*Samson*). Carissimi was well-known in England, the collection of his works by Dean Aldrich being the finest outside Italy. His most celebrated work was *Jephtha,* and the chorus used in *Samson* had been printed 70 or 80 years before in Kircher's renowned *Musurgia.* Steffani's motet *Qui diligit Mariam,* thought to have been used in 'Music spread' (*Solomon*) had been specially presented to the Academy of Antient Musick, of which at the time of presentation Steffani was president. Indeed, when there was a split in the Academy some years before, the possession of Steffani's motets formed one of the subjects of contention. Of some suites of Mattheson, a theme from which was used in a suite of Handel's, published apparently in 1742, but probably written and in circulation much earlier, it happens to be recorded that in 1714 Handel found them just issued from a London press, and played them in public, to show his esteem for the author.†

The only way of avoiding the general conclusion would be to execute a *volte-face,* and call these resemblances accidental. But there are far too many to allow us to make

---

*A. Pirro, *L'Esthétique de Jean-Sebastien Bach,* p. 395, with a reference to Spitta. [ii. 492]

† Hawkins, v. 253.

accident responsible for all. We may regard it as certain that Handel's open use of themes passed unchallenged in England, as it had passed unchallenged in Germany. When Mattheson's *Ehrenpforte* reached England with its open references in a notice written *ex professo* in honour of Handel—to whom, by the bye, Mattheson had dedicated his *Fingersprache* (May, 1735)—it would arouse no surprise in the minds of Dr. Pepusch and the throng of Germans in London.* And there is no reason to suppose that any more objection would be taken to Handel's selecting seven or eight themes from Muffat for his *Ode on St. Cecilia's Day* than to Bach doing the same thing by *Almira*. But let the admission be made with all speed that to take a theme is a very different thing from taking a large portion or the whole of a movement.

III.

And yet, viewing the matter in relation to a composer of the front rank, must we pronounce the difference really vital? Such a composer has acquired a technique, a dexterity, a sense of fitness, such that, provided he has found a good theme or initial idea, time and labour alone are required for him to produce something of higher artistic value than the compositions of less gifted men. 'Only give me a theme,' said Haydn, if I remember rightly, 'and I will work it out according to the rules of art.' The beautiful, the felicitous idea in his smaller neighbour's possession is what the front-rank man might naturally covet. And it was just these ideas that in the time of Handel and Bach might be utilised by other composers, the ideas being sometimes both beautiful and extensive. The theme of Bach's G minor fugue, whatever may have been its origin, is very long and important.† Hear again

---

* Burney was acquainted with the *Ehrenpforte*.
† See above, p. 54.

what Spitta says about about another theme : ' Does not this broad deliberate subject [quotation of theme], with its echo-like diminuendo to *piano* and *pianissimo,* sound as if it had been born of space and died away again, shuddering into infinitude ? ' (i, 572). This is a theme taken by Bach from Handel's *Almira,* 'Gönne nach den Thränen-güssen.'

Finding then Handel adapting with little alteration a chorus of Graun's, we ask ourselves : ' Why did he not simply take over the theme, which gives the character to the movement, and apply a fresh development, which would have resulted in a chorus decidedly superior to Graun's if he had taken a little trouble ? ' And this question we are the more entitled to ask, because that is precisely the course he actually did take later with one of these 'Graun' choruses ; its subject or subjects he introduced into 'Mourn ye afflicted children' (*Judas*), a chorus to which most people would accord an unequivocal preference. Again, had he written *currente calamo* a new development, which would take little more time than the actual labour of transcription, he might have produced something approximately as good as Graun's, certainly good enough for his public, and good enough for any hopes of advantage he may have entertained. Why, we may ask, this time with Kerl's canzona in our minds, if with just a little more trouble you can raise from a foreign cutting a ' Gloire de Dijon ' rose, why transplant a cabbage ? We are called to realms of romance, when we are bidden to think of Handel as running such tremendous risks for such infinitesimal profit. He must have been another Lord Scroop ; not the slightest instance was there why he should do treason. However, Mr. Sedley Taylor and many others apparently will have it so, and we must proceed with the examination of their reasons, but as applicable now to a few movements, some dozen in all, where the extent of the obligation may markedly exceed the common practices of the time.

CHAPTER VIII.

HAWKINS AND BURNEY.

I.

THE question is, why none of the borrowings from Graun, Muffat, Kerl, Habermann, and Clari are named by Hawkins, and only one case (Clari)—and that perhaps of the least formal importance—by Burney. How is their silence to be explained? To Mainwaring no importance seems to be attached, and rightly so. He was but a theological student, 25 years old, who hastily compiled a biography for a bookseller. The work is quite short, and more than half the space devoted to actual biography is filled with a sketch of Handel's career before he reached England in 1710. Though Mainwaring inserts a story about Bononcini meeting the boy Handel at Berlin, he says nothing whatever about the madrigal. Throughout the work, which appeared without his name, he makes no profession of deep research; however, somebody, probably Smith junior, must have supplied him with a fairly comprehensive catalogue of Handel's works, a few significant omissions notwithstanding. The book is eked out by general remarks and appreciations, which while affecting, as was customary, the impartial and the oracular, betray little knowledge except in the case of some duets and trios; and even here, it is significant to observe, he knows nothing whatever of a number of duets, written *circa* 1740—1745, although these were utilised for *The Messiah* and other oratorios.

For all that, Mr. Sedley Taylor would have done better to examine more carefully a passage from which he extracts a few words. Here it is :—

'However it is very remarkable that some persons on whom the finest modulations would have little or no effect, have been greatly struck with Handel's Chorusses. This is probably owing to *that grandeur of conception, which predominates in them;* and which, as *coming purely from Nature,* is the more strongly and more generally felt.'

By confining his attention to the words I have italicised and which he has quoted, Mr. Taylor has pressed the passage into his service. Yet surely Mainwaring is simply speaking of the effect produced on the unlearned music-lover, the 'direct appeal' of Handel's choruses. The same sentiment differently expressed might be found in any modern biographer; it is pretty much what Spitta has said in the passage quoted p. 41, and yet Spitta would have learnt little that was fresh to him from Mr. Taylor's pages. However, as observed above, it is not on the silence of Mainwaring but on the silence of Hawkins and Burney that stress is laid.

Now it is perfectly true that if Hawkins and Burney had written special studies of Handel's life, and had possessed the combined merits of a Boswell and a Prynne, had eagerly questioned everyone, and taken care to omit nothing, their silence would be very formidable. Without being exactly great men, they were men with abilities distinctly above the average. But in reality they were universal historians, men confronted with masses of material, often intractable, to the bulk of which they must turn like Nelson a blind eye; else would their task be unending. What then were their special characteristics, their studies, their opportunities?

II.

Sir John Hawkins (1719—1789) was by profession a lawyer. In 1753 he made a wealthy marriage, and was by this enabled to devote himself to his favourite hobby of music. He purchased part of the musical collection of

Dr. Pepusch, who had died in 1752. He was Chairman of the Middlesex justices for several years, and was knighted on presenting an address to the king. Besides his *History of Music* (5 vols., 1776), which covered the whole musical field, he engaged in other literary work, contributing, *inter alia,* papers to the *Gentleman's Magazine*, editing the *Complete Angler,* and writing a biography (1787) of Dr. Johnson, whose executor he was. He claims to have called occasionally on Handel, but there is nothing to indicate particular intimacy;* indeed it is noticeable how faithfully he follows Mainwaring's account with its blunders 'gross as a mountain, open, palpable.' The earlier parts of Sir John's History would naturally occupy most of his time at first, and were those in which Dr. Pepusch's collections would assist him most; when he came to write of Handel some time after 1770, he would be writing of matters (from our point of view) 20, 30, or 40 years old. His work was eclectic; borrowings from Clari, Graun, Muffat, and Habermann might have been mentioned in the same way as the borrowing from Carissimi, had the names of those composers found their way into his work at all, which is not the case, so far as I have observed. Kerl's canzona he inserts—possibly from Dr. Pepusch's collection—without naming Handel, but for a reason to be mentioned later† it was not all likely that Handel's connexion with it should have reached his ear. The use of Graun would for practical purposes be nearly 40 years old. Unless the borrowings had at the time produced vigorous attacks, Hawkins might easily never have heard a word of them, for his position would be that of a comparative outsider, until Handel's career was practically ended.

And if he had heard anything, what would he have heard? A colourless vague remark that 'Egypt was glad' (*Israel*) was 'taken from' some piece from Kerl, who might

---

* Hawkins was, according to Dr. Johnson, an 'unclubable' man.
† p. 92.

figure, however, unblushingly as Krieger or Kusser—few
people carry names with ease and certainty.   When narrat-
ing indifferent things we take no trouble to define exact
extent with precision. 'Taken from' is sufficient. I have
observed, by the bye, that 'verbatim' and 'note for note'
are gloriously elastic terms.   Sir John, I imagine, might
have heard a story about *Joshua* and Telemann, and never
suspected—how should he?—that it had aught to do with
Jephtha and Habermann, whose masses perchance adorned
his own library.   Nay, he might actually possess a copy
of Graun's *Passion,* and be told under his own roof of the
use of Graun's work in *The Triumph of Time and Truth,*
and yet never become enlightened.   How could this
happen? With the greatest of ease.   His informant had
only to do as Crotch did in one of his notes, to speak of
Graun's work as a *Mass*. 'You don't mean a *Passion,* I
suppose? I have a *Passion* of his upstairs.'   The informant is an average man.   He probably believes he was
told *Mass*; anyhow, he is not ready to be corrected by Sir
John Hawkins; 'No, no, a *Mass,* a *Mass*.'   The point is of
no particular importance; they are chatting over their wine
by a good fire; the conversation quickly flows in fresh
channels.   Perhaps some months afterwards Sir John is
reminded of Graun's *Passion;* he takes it down, and turns
it over.   Wasn't there some tale of Handel's honouring
Graun by adapting one of his choruses, and hadn't he
himself at the time a vague idea that this *Passion* might be
meant?   He will just compare it with *Theodora,* of which
he might conceivably have a manuscript copy; he has a
few minutes to spare.   No, he can't find any resemblance;
the other man had made no blunder; that is, if there was
any grain of truth at all in his story.   It might take months
to discover the real facts; is he to make some vague remark,
and have that 'clever dog' Burney, who is also writing a
history, expose his ignorance?   He is conscious of having
been out of his depth throughout the greater part of his

sketch,* and of having written much that he would not care to stand to. He lets the point drop, all the more because his scheme does not require him to mention Graun at all.

Of omissions and blunders Hawkins has rich sheaves. Two examples may be given. Of Handel's *Alceste* (which was really written in 1750, the music being afterwards utilised for the *Choice of Hercules,* 1751), he gives an account of the origin, and says that 'Handel afterwards adapted this music to Dryden's Song for St. Cecilia's Day'—which was written in 1739.

Another blunder is that noted by Chrysander (i, 342) concerning a quotation by Hawkins from Mattheson. Perhaps a sufficient approximation to it will be made if we conceive the terms of opprobrium 'Tom fool' and 'Stick' gaining dignity as 'Mr. Thomas Fool' and '—— Strick Esq.'

Only haste, however, will infer that because Hawkins does not mention a fact, he was necessarily ignorant of it. By a passage from Mattheson this point is brought into relief. He has told us in the *Ehrenpforte* (1740) that Handel used themes from operas written by himself. One of these must have been the fugue theme in the overture to *Agrippina,* taken from Mattheson's *Cleopatra* (1704). Yet in his *Der Vollkommene Kapellmeister* (1739) he introduced this theme to dilate upon it, without making any reference whatever to Handel.

* As was unavoidable; the subject was too vast for one man; indeed modern historians taking periods far less extensive must occasionally have similar suspicions.

III.

Charles Burney (1726—1814) came to London to study music in 1744. He played for a short time in Handel's orchestra, and has given an account of the rehearsals, which were often held at Carlton House, the residence of the Prince of Wales; but he was, of course, too young yet to penetrate further than the outer courts. His attention, however, was quickly diverted to other branches, particularly opera, and in a few years he won a position of some dignity. Weak health, nevertheless, induced him to take a post as organist at King's Lynn, and there he resided till 1760, his occasional visits to London being undertaken, it would appear, mainly to hear the new operas. On his return to London his labours were arduous, his time being mostly occupied in the teaching of a large number of pupils. In 1771 he published *The present state of music in France and Italy,* and in 1773 *The present state of music in Germany, the Netherlands, and United Provinces, etc.;* these works, the fruit of journeys on the continent, gave Dr. Johnson the hint for his *Journey to the Hebrides.* Between 1776 and 1789 appeared his *History of Music,* the last volume containing most of his references to Handel.

In his spare time Burney chiefly affected the society of literary men and the foreign musicians who visited England.* Of his fellow-musicians of English birth he could have known little; indeed we may without unkindness suspect a slight touch of disdain in his attitude. Of foreign and particularly of Italian music he was a warm admirer; even Handel seems to have sunk a little in his regard, until he actually visited Italy.† Afterwards he threw himself ardently into the revival of Handel's works, and wrote the account of the Handel commemoration, 1785. It was only after the careful examination of Handel's operas

---

* For a brilliant account of Burney on the social side, see Lord Macaulay's 'Review of the Diary and Letters of Madame d'Arblay.'

† 'Tour in France and Italy,' p. 164.

for the purposes of his history that he thoroughly realised their immense superiority over all other operas—Gluck, of course, not entering into the comparison.

Looking back on these data we perceive that he was not in London when Kerl's canzona was used (1738) nor at any 'Graun' period, 1736-7 and 1757. The borrowings from Muffat in *St. Cecilia's Day* occurred in 1739; the borrowings from Habermann in 1752, when he was at King's Lynn. Really the only borrowings of importance when he was in London, and sufficiently prominent to be likely to hear of such things, are those in *Theodora* from Clari and, in a less degree, from Muffat. And, as it happens, though this may be accidental, it is the borrowings from Clari that he mentions. Muffat and Habermann find no place in his History, nor yet in the account of his travels. Of Graun and Kerl, in connexion with those failures *Il Trionfo* and *Israel,* no one was likely to be talking when Burney came to London.

From the vagueness of his reference to Clari it is evident that Burney had taken no trouble to examine the point personally. How are we to account for this? Doubtless in part because he had only twenty-four hours in the day, and had far more important matters (to his thinking) to attend to. His interests could not be all-embracing. When his daughter told him that she proposed to bring out a novel (*Evelina*) anonymously, if he would grant permission, 'he only stared, burst out a-laughing, kissed her, gave her leave to do as she liked, and never even asked the name of her work.'* The finishing of his own labours preoccupied him, and, be it observed, a historian never *will* finish his work, if he is continually pursuing fresh hares. 'Thou shalt renounce, renounce.' The cruel difficulties in clearing up obscurities would be borne in upon Burney. He was, as we know, specially interested in opera; now Handel had brought out at his theatre

* Macaulay.

between 1730 and 1740, besides his well-known operas, about a dozen, as to which Burney could not discover, except in one or two cases, whether they were original operas or pasticcios, and, if pasticcios, whose the music was. We now know that they were pasticcios, though apparently the composers are not named—another case of non-acknowledgment? Perhaps Burney could have gained enlightenment by applying to Smith junior; but even had the idea occurred to him, Smith was no longer in London, his address might be difficult to obtain, the whole thing would take time, etc., etc.

Any floating story that might conceivably reach Burney would be 'of doubtful authenticity.' How quickly are facts forgotten, with what alert celerity do they suffer modification! 'The price of' accuracy is 'eternal vigilance,' and it is most difficult to be eternally vigilant. I doubt whether by 1780 any traditional story about any one of our five composers would be in a happier plight than the lovable story of the prim man in *Pickwick,* about 'a great public character, whose name he had forgotten, making a particularly happy reply to another eminent and illustrious individual, whom he had never been able to identify.' The precise point of the anecdote, moreover, just then escaped the prim man's memory 'although he had been in the habit of telling the story with great applause for the last ten years.' How many can name the non-Mozartian elements in *Don Giovanni* and *Figaro*? How many readers of Jahn remember that according to one authority Mozart thrust into an early mass a whole movement from some deceased Italian composer?* How many students of literature have ever heard of Wordsworth's insertion among his own sonnets of one whole sonnet by some unnamed author? Wordsworth only

---

* Jahn, iii, 376 note. Sievers, who heard it from a Kapellmeister at Ferrara, confirmed by Santini, had forgotten the key of the mass and the name of the composer. Of course he would forget them.

mentions the fact in a note at the end of the volume. Of the sonnet I cannot recall one word; my copy of Wordsworth has been temporarily mislaid as I write; but by wading through Wordsworth's notes a 'not impossible he' may find it, if he chooses. Now why should an open insertion of some foreign movement by Handel be any more firmly riveted in the memory of his contemporaries?

Fortunately we can test the value of this 'silence' argument by some crucial instances :—

(1) Burney's final volume was issued, we remember, in 1789. Now at least as early as 1780 vivid interest had been aroused in some musical circles in London by a manuscript having some references to 'Urio.' Its connexion with Handel's *Dettingen Te Deum* could not have escaped notice, as this Te Deum was well-known and performed annually at St. Paul's Cathedral. And what does Burney say about it? Not a syllable.

(2) Burney had mentioned in print the use of Clari. Crotch had publicly in 1831 drawn attention to the use of Muffat. Now Sir George Macfarren had taken part in the controversy about the 'Erba' *Magnificat*. In 1873, in the course of an article about *Theodora* he pointed out a slight and quite trivial resemblance between 'Sweet rose and lily' and Bononcini's 'Per la gloria,' and expressed further his bewilderment over the inexplicable title 'Trio' in the Overture. He could not, then, have had the faintest idea of the use of Clari and Muffat; he would have learnt with surprise that the 'Trio' is so-called, because it was taken from a 'Trio' in Muffat's *Componimenti*.

(3) Crotch in 1831 made public mention of Graun. Privately he gave full details as to the use of a chorus from Graun's *Passion* in *The Triumph of Time and Truth* as 'Ere to dust.' Moreover, Graun's chorus had appeared in print prior to 1831 in Latrobe's collection. Now in 1871 Professor Prout was no novice in the subject. In that year he wrote articles, in no perfunctory spirit, about

Urio, Stradella, and Handel. Yet of Crotch's statement he seems to have known nothing, though he had independently noted the connexion between the two choruses, Graun's and Handel's. Dr. Chrysander in 1857 was equally unconscious; that which had been freely talked about in the time of Crotch, which must have been easily verifiable in the (probably) not few libraries which contained both Latrobe and *The Triumph of Time and Truth* slipped from the general consciousness and required rediscovery.

These instances have been chosen because they are freed from the suspicion of being fetched from afar. Every man's experience will multiply such cases indefinitely; but these were knocking at our gates. And remark that though Crotch himself seems to have regarded such things as open quotations, yet many in his time did not share his view. It was in spite of a certain piquancy of scandal that the knowledge died out.

CHAPTER IX.

ENEMIES.

LET us begin by casting to the ends of the earth all idea of secrecy. We are not now to consider what might have happened if Handel's opponents had made able or lucky discoveries of things he had tried to conceal; we are trying to gauge what was likely to happen if he borrowed with the openness of innocence, as openly as Berlioz borrowed a Hungarian march not in its older form, but in that to which the original idea had been quite recently moulded by a known composer; as openly as in later days Sir Hubert Parry introduced Chopin's Funeral March into his *Pied Piper of Hamelin*.

What reason for thinking themselves aggrieved would invade the minds of Handel's enemies? That sense of being taken in, which quickened, we may suspect, the resentment of the Academy against Bononcini, would be quite absent here. His antagonists were not in the least likely to be nervous about possible misunderstandings in future days, after he had 'outsoared the shadow' of their night. Could they be wroth because he stole surreptitiously, and then meanly aggravated the offence by telling people what he had done? At the utmost they could only accuse him of want of originality, and were they ever in a position to make such a charge? In the opinion of Plato's Socrates* to prosecute your father gracefully was a very difficult task, and it is equally difficult to arraign the originality of a man, whose compositions you find it profitable to use.

Whose was the music of that particularly successful

* Euthyphro.

pasticcio *Lucio Vero* (1747)?   Handel's.   Who had
formerly written (as *Alessandro*) the successful *Roxana*
(1743)?   Handel.   Who had lauded Handel's abilities up
to 1733?   His infuriated enemies.   Whose air had Dr.
Pepusch taught to his parrot?   Handel's.   The fact is,
nobody seriously doubted Handel's great genius, however
irritating his proceedings might be.   Hasse, had it been
necessary, could have thrown light on that point, when
he was enticed over to oppose Handel in 1734.   The
Duchess of Marlborough, Bononcini's former patroness,
subscribed to *Atalanta*, 1736; Dr. Pepusch, often credited
with hostility, subscribed regularly for six or more copies
of the operas.   There is a story told by Mainwaring and
Hawkins that Lord Middlesex, the head of the opera, paid
Handel £1000 for *Faramondo* and *Alessandro Severo*
(1737-8).   Burney, it is true, followed by Rockstro, rejects
this story on grounds not quite sufficient,* and Chrysander
may be right in substituting Heidegger's name for that of
Lord Middlesex.   But in any case Heidegger had been
associated with the opposition from 1734 to 1737.   Whether
in 1738 these aristocrats were still leagued with him, or
whether the opera was now entirely his own venture, it is
clear that Heidegger must have relied on the party of the
nobility for his subscribers; and he would not have
brought out Handel's works in 1738, as he certainly did,
along with operas by Pescetti and Veracini, if Handel's
music or personality had been very distasteful.   Probably
the opponents were for a time a little repentant of having
reduced Handel to bankruptcy and mental affliction in
1737.   They seem to have made overtures to him only
to meet with a haughty rejection.†   That the quarrel was

---

* See a letter of Mrs. Delany's, Nov. 28, 1739 : 'Lord Middlesex is the
chief undertaker'; which shows that his practical management of the opera
began before the date 1741, assigned by Burney.

† Mainwaring, who is practically confirmed by the writer of a letter in
1741 quoted by Chrysander, iii, 140.

never regarded as beyond adjustment is made probable by Handel's finding it necessary in 1742 to contradict the report that he was to manage the operas in the coming season.*

It must be remembered again that the borrowings arraigned began practically with the *Wedding Anthem* for the Prince of Wales, April, 1736. Now from 1736 onwards Handel was supported, not only by the King, but by the Prince of Wales, who was the leader of the parliamentary opposition, and had been accounted previously the head of the rival opera undertaking. From 1736 the Prince and Princess were frequent patrons of Handel's concerts, and his rehearsals were often held at their residence. Who was likely to print silly attacks on a man thus doubly guarded? And who was likely to attack a man supported by Pope, Fielding and Smollett? Up to 1742 there would be room for the luckless wight in the fourth book of the Dunciad.

But we must also remember the absence of journalistic attacks of any kind whatsoever. It is true that there appeared a nominal onslaught in the *Craftsman,* April 7th, 1733, bearing the signature P—lo R—li [Paolo Rolli]; but that was fictitious in every respect, being really an able attack on Walpole's Excise Bill by some political writer who used the musical quarrels simply as a cover. Every detail, quite meaningless or fatuous with respect to Handel, applies with telling force to Walpole. Chrysander has pointed out many illustrations, the most palpable being the audience 'of about 260'; *i.e.,* the 266 supporters of the Excise Bill's first reading. [Rolli, by the bye, was the librettist of Handel's last opera *Deidamia* (1740).] There is some good-humoured banter of the 'man-mountain' in a pamphlet of 1751, but from the

* 'The report that the Direction of the opera here next winter is committed to my care is groundless. The gentlemen who have undertaken to meddle with Harmony, cannot agree, and are quite in confusion.' Handel to Jennens, Sept. 9, 1742.

extracts one would judge the whole satire really directed against the cheap methods of Italian opera-writers, who had discovered the art of learning to compose in 24 hours.* Otherwise we hear of nothing except caricatures, such as that of Goupy, in which Handel's genius is expressly recognised :

> 'There dwells a soul of soft desires
> And all that harmony inspires.'

The contest between Handel and the nobility was a contest between two managements, and was conducted on commercial lines. It was no matter of art, and why should the nobility give Handel a splendid advertisement by making a silly attack on him? They alone would be the sufferers, for it would naturally pack Handel's house. So far as they were concerned Handel was merely a rival *entrepreneur*. Both sides competed in offering entertainments to the public, a public, that is, which cared very little who provided the music. Burney remarks that it was quite a rare thing for the name of the composer to be mentioned in the advertisements. It happened exceptionally in the case of one opera by Hasse, for then it was thought his name might attract. But for the most part an opera was an opera, relying on its own merits rather than on the name of the composer. Indeed three times out of five the composer was a syndicate. The airs of *Orfeo,* says Burney, 'were chiefly selected from the works of Hasse, Vinci, Araja and Porpora.' This is quite an average specimen as to numbers. Now supposing it were known that Handel introduced a couple of choruses of Graun's, more or less altered, into his entertainment (for so it was advertised) *Il Trionfo* (1737)—one of them having been previously used, as everyone knew, in the Wedding Anthem of Prince Frederick—how could his opponents have the colossal impudence to object, when they were pitting four or five composers against him?

* Chrysander, ii, 328.

Would they haggle over 'acknowledgments?' The airs
were 'chiefly,' says Burney, which means, I suppose,
that the names of the other composers were not thought
worthy of mention; in a selection of airs from *Orpheus*,
printed by Walsh, there are several unadorned by the
composer's name.* Would the nobility be deeply stirred
because Handel, constructing an oratorio primarily in
connexion with the Academy of Antient Musick, adapted
an organ canzona of Kerl's, which was probably well-
known to the members? Yet it is against these three
choruses above all that modern criticism has hurled its
thunderbolts. How could his antagonists criticise as not
original the man whose single-handed might kept the field
against their syndicates? And if they fastidiously required
incessant unaided fertility from Handel, why did they not
fall foul of those numerous pasticcios which he constructed
as stop-gaps till the new operas were ready?

There is another consideration. You would expect
attacks, you say. Yes, but *when* would you expect them?
We can run lightly from 1736 to 1757 in the fraction of a
second; for contemporaries these represented 21 weary
years. At no one time would it seem worth while to the
most stupid and rancorous of enemies to make a public
attack on Handel. *Il Trionfo* would not furnish material
for a pamphlet, or even a newspaper letter—which no
editor, however, was likely to print. When two years
later the 'Kerl' appeared, pulses would beat steadily.
When in 1739 and 1740 Handel used themes from Muffat's
work in his *St. Cecilia's Day* and his *Concertos*, no one
was likely to invite attention to Handel's immense
superiority. And in later years what would be the point
in objections to things which had so long passed unchallenged?

* When into a revival of *Poro* (1736) Handel introduced four Italian
airs, unchanged except for some alterations in the words, the libretto
asterisked them as 'not by Mr. Handel,' but did not trouble to name the
composers. See Chrysander, ii, 246.

After all, commercial or political rivalries are subject to an unwritten ethical code. You may have set up a shop and tried to take away the customers of the emporium over the way, but you do not therefore feel justified in printing attacks on his private character, not even if your assertions can be proved, and will bring you in safety through an action for libel. Political warfare, though conducted with the most unsparing invective, acknowledges similar restrictions. Handel's opponents would not blindly snatch at any stick, wherewith to belabour him. Theirs was no Bess o' Bedlam fury.* At heart everybody would have a great admiration for him. *Lucio Vero* (1747) was, in the words of the opera company, probably 'the most exquisite composition of harmony ever offered to the public . . . Mr. Handel is acknowledged (universally) so great a master of the lyre . . .' His pride and obstinacy were, no doubt, very tiresome; he was like Jock o' Dawston Cleugh 'a camsteary chield and fasheous about marches,'† but for all that the Dandie Dinmonts of his day would hesitate to 'wrang' him. There is a pretty story in Coxe's Anecdotes about Handel's deputy, Smith junior, and Lord Middlesex. Smith produced a musical drama in 1754 at Garrick's theatre. Before the performance Garrick accosted Smith in great perturbation; Lord Middlesex had taken forty places in the boxes; what could that mean except the deliberate ruining of the drama? Poor Smith was puzzled, for Lord Middlesex had always been extremely kind to him. But his doubts continued till the actual performance, when to Garrick's astonishment those forty seats in the boxes were the foremost in the applause.

* A tale that in 1741 his advertisements were torn from the walls is expressly attributed by the source of information to the baser sort, not to the leaders among his opponents.

† Scott. *Guy Mannering.*

CHAPTER X.

The Counter-Argument.

I.

This 'argumentum a silentio,' then, adds its mite to the common experience, which condemns such arguments as untrustworthy. Before we present the counter-arguments, the results of the previous chapters may with some advantage be summarised. (1) To other composers also the arguments of Mr. Sedley Taylor would have their application. (2) The escapade of Bononcini is devoid of all relevance for our purpose; moreover, the sensitiveness of the English public on such points is quite insufficiently attested. (3) The 'non-acknowledgment' argument rears its crest not against openness towards contemporaries, but against openness towards posterity, and on examination loses all its plausibility. (4) The silence of Hawkins, Burney, and Handel's contemporaries is by no means the total silence which Mr. Sedley Taylor has suggested, and the incompleteness of their information seems pretty much what we should have expected. (5) For many reasons Handel's opponents were not likely to print attacks on open borrowings. It may be as well to direct attention once more to the patronage of the Prince of Wales, who had formerly been at the head of his opponents, but just at the beginning of the period which interests us discontinued his hostility.

1. Let us turn now to the opposing arguments, and take first those derived from general considerations. The theory, let it not be forgotten, is that Handel worked in secret with as few associates as possible. Now when we consider the immense amount of work done by his secre-

tary, Smith senior, the notion of his being kept in ignorance will be seen to be inadmissible. A strong point, therefore, is made by Mr. Balfour,* when he brings forward the quarrel between Handel and Smith, which is described by Archdeacon Coxe on the authority of Smith junior. Had Smith senior been cognisant of discreditable secrets, how could Handel have dared to quarrel with him? Mr. Sedley Taylor notes this argument, but makes no attempt to meet it. And, in truth, this is not surprising, for what possible answer can be given? *Ex hypothesi* the secrets were such as Handel's enemies would have been very glad to learn, and such as would have injured seriously his reputation. The risks in a quarrel would have been too great.

2. Whatever the consequences of detection would have been, small or great, Handel must have run that risk for little or no profit. It is not only that a very slight expenditure of time, as remarked above,† would have put him in line with customary practices; there is the curious fact that he must have set no store by some of the chief of his acquisitions. We find that, after the first performance, the 'Kerl' chorus 'Egypt was glad' was *struck out,* and apparently never performed again during Handel's lifetime.‡ And one of the 'Graun' choruses in *Il Trionfo* (1737) finds no place in the English version, 1757. No fear of detection could have caused the excision, for the chorus retained was far the more likely to be recognised by anyone acquainted with Graun's work. So that in two of the three leading cases Handel either thought very little of the compositions from the first, or recognised quickly that they won neither credit nor popularity.

3. A third consideration is that the particular works of Kerl, Muffat, and Habermann were in print. This may

* *Essays and Addresses,* p. 155.
† p. 74.
‡ Chrysander, iii. 91.

possibly be true also of Clari's duets; in fact ' Grove's
Dictionary' s.v. Clari makes the statement, while Burney
dates their printing at 1720. If so, only the work of
Graun was unprinted so far as is known, and *Passions*
very seldom went to the press, though they might circulate
widely. And remark that the non-printing of this one
work does not in the least affect the value of the
inference based on the printing of the others; *their* circulation would suffer no shrinkage in consequence.

4. The next observation is that Handel's method was
precisely what a man fearing detection would have avoided
like the leaving of finger-prints. He troubles not to place
the two choruses of Graun in different oratorios; no, he
quite makes a point of crowding material from the same
source largely into the same work; Muffat into *St. Cecilia's
Day,* Clari into *Theodora,* Habermann into *Jephtha.* Any
suspicion, that might have been aroused in the minds of
listeners or purchasers, would have found its confirmation
at once. Really he must have *wished* to be found out,
like a Galatea, ' [Quae] fugit ad salices, et se cupit ante
videri.'

5. It may be said, it has been said, that England was
so isolated in the world of music, that there was practically little risk in any case. Mr. Sedley Taylor has not
put forward this statement, I think, and a statement of
greater wildness could not easily be invented. As Paris
nowadays to Americans, so was London in those days to
continental musicians. Bononcini, Ariosti, Domenico
Scarlatti, Hasse, Gluck, Geminiani, Veracini, and others
visited England in Handel's time.* Nowhere else was
the pay so good, and nowhere, in Mattheson's opinion,
were there better judges of music. Substituting Vienna

* Or examine a dictionary, say Riemann's, for foreign musicians visiting
England, 1710—1760. Abel, Abos, Ariosti, Arrigoni, Astorga, J. C. Bach,
Barsanti, Bernacchi, Bernardi, etc.

for Paris we might apply to the musical world that description of London (1738):

'The common shore of Paris and of Rome.'

Composers and singers, Germans Italians and Nether-
landers jostled one another in the streets of the West
End, a district inhabited then by perhaps 100,000 souls,
a district which embraced almost all the 'classical' musical
life of the kingdom.   And not only was London the most
unfavourable spot—Vienna perhaps ranking next—but of
all living composers Handel was the most likely to be
detected, for a much larger proportion of his work was
printed than of any other European musician.   True, few
of his choruses were printed; he must have tried to get
contemporary reputation from borrowed choruses, which
would only be heard and quickly forgotten.*   But among
the printed works are a few which easily lent themselves
to identification, for instance a march in *Joshua* and a trio
in the overture to *Theodora*.   Any visitor from Vienna
could compare Muffat's *Componimenti* with these works to
his heart's content.   And the most likely to be recognised
of the borrowings from Habermann in *Jephtha* occurred
in a song that was printed.

II.

Let us direct our attention now to the special circumstances in the prominent cases, observing that the 'secrecy'
theory requires, not the bold venture and lucky success in
one case, but in all cases; each successive daring coup
was triumphant.   It will be assumed that these are genuine,
though, strictly speaking, some formal objections might be
raised.   It might be suggested for instance that the themes
in Keiser's *Octavia* were derived from Handel's lost *Nero*,

---

* It is curious, however, to find an otherwise unprinted chorus from a
'Chandos' Anthem, in an abbreviated form, in a work published at Venice
in 1765—the only non-Italian example in the book.   Chrysander i, 463.

Keiser having taken over the themes when he took over the libretto in an altered form; indeed Keiser's preface to *La fedeltà coronata* (Chrysander, i, 131) might be thought to hint at this. It might also be objected that just as Hasse's *Demofonte* was credited to Graun, because a copy of it existed in his handwriting,* so the 'Brunswick' *Passion* might simply be a copy of some lost work of Handel's made by Graun.† However, no objections will be raised here. It will be assumed also that the use of Keiser was no secret, so that the case of Graun's *Passion* may be considered first. Let us look more closely at the circumstances, 1736-7.

The first question, of course, must be this : how did Handel get the manuscript? Had he, like Macbeth, 'a servant fee'd' in the house of each promising young composer? Did he make journeys in disguise to the continent besides those mentioned in the newspapers? Did he send his secretary, Smith, also *incognito,* on roving commissions? Handel himself was of marked figure, and well-known, and unless Smith concealed his personality, his connexion with Handel would mark him out. If he openly selected works for Handel, the fact would not be stifled. It would be known that one of the two or three copies of Graun's work had gone to Handel; unless, indeed, the work was very popular, and then what a risk would be run !

However, most people, remembering that Brunswick is only some 35 miles from Hanover, where George II. and his suite stayed from May to October, 1735, and that the borrowings begin January, 1736, will be content to suppose

---

* Herr Reinach. 'S.I.M.G.,' i, 461.

† By the bye, if Graun went to Rheinsberg in 1735, according to the accepted statement, he went before Prince Frederick (the Great), who took up his residence there, Aug. 6, 1736. 'Grove's' statement that Graun's brother went into Frederick's service at Rheinsberg in 1728 is absolutely impossible. The former might be explained as meaning Ruppin, a few miles from Rheinsberg; yet Frederick seems to have been stationed at Dantzic in the second half of 1735.

the manuscript came over at the same time as his Majesty.*
Now a manuscript that is thought worth taking to England
is probably thought worth talking about, and worthy of
being shown to those interested in music. If it came
over in this natural way, many others besides Handel
would have seen it, or heard of it. Quite a goodly number
would require bribing. Nevertheless some one, no doubt,
may be more fortunate in discovering a possible method of
secret transference, and we may consider the likelihood of
Handel's secretly introducing, almost unchanged, the first
chorus of Graun's work into the anthem for the wedding
(April 27th, 1736) of Frederick, Prince of Wales, who
would be likely to know Graun in his boyhood, to Princess
Augusta of Saxe-Gotha, who had recently been staying
near Hanover, perhaps at Brunswick, being possibly a
pupil of Graun's, the whole court having recently returned
from Hanover. There was the largest possible chance of
detection, and absolutely no hope of profit. And in the
previous air Handel had also introduced an instrumental
phrase from Graun, which might have stimulated dormant
recollections. The chorus 'Lo thus shall the man' is the
same as that used in *Il Trionfo* and *The Triumph of Time*
as 'Ere to dust.'

But Handel introduced also a very recognisable idea
from the *Passion* into *Atalanta*, May, 1736, an opera
intended also to celebrate the wedding, and printed at once
by subscription. Now were Handel's operas unknown in
Brunswick? On the contrary, during Graun's stay in that
town as many of Handel's operas as of his own were
performed, and far more than those of any other composer. † *Ottone, Giulio Cesare, Riccardo, Admeto, Poro,
Partenope,* delighted the Brunswickers, and some of these
were repeated as late as 1739. Whether *Atalanta* was

---

* Was the *Passion* music used at the funeral of Duke Ferdinand of
Brunswick, September 3, 1735? Such adaptations were common, I fancy.
  † Chrysander.

ever performed there, I do not know; the latest of the
above operas was *Partenope* (1731); but Handel was at
any rate quite powerless to prevent performances, as it
was from the printed collection of airs that operas were
often staged, the recitatives being supplied by local composers. So that, just at the time when he was secretly
introducing the chorus, he was advertising his knowledge
of Graun's work *urbi et orbi*. He did the same thing next
year with *Giustino*. And having thus put any one who
might be acquainted with the *Passion* on the *qui vive*, he,
secretly if you will, but surely in a very sporting spirit,
introduced the two choruses into *Il Trionfo* two months
after the production of *Giustino*. The most stony-hearted
curmudgeon will not refuse a slight tribute of admiration.

Taking next the 'Kerl' we find from the 'Denkmäler
der Tonkunst' that the canzona must have been esteemed,
for it was reprinted in a collection of movements by Pas-
quini, Poglietti, and Kerl, issued by Roger at Amsterdam
in 1704. And this particular collection must itself have
been popular, for it was reprinted by Mortier at Amsterdam, and (with some additions) by Walsh at London.
The dates of these editions are not known; whether
Walsh's was issued in Handel's lifetime is uncertain; it
cannot have been long after his death, for the younger
Walsh retired a few years later. Hawkins' reproduction
of our canzona, if we may judge from its curious variations, was not printed from any of the editions, but from
some manuscript copy. From the fact of his happening
to select this, it is likely that it was known separately from
the rest. It is in the Phrygian mode, and might be
popular with Dr. Pepusch and the Antient Academy. At
any rate these would be the most likely people in England
to know the work; yet we find that the Academy gave
performances of part of *Israel* a few weeks after its first
production, so that they must have had access to the
score. Indeed we may conjecture that the oratorio origi-

nated in a proposed revival of an early *Magnificat* of Handel's by the Academy. And those who vaguely conceive of Kerl as obscure may be urged to reflect on such visitors to England as De Fesch, who had been an organist at Antwerp, and came thence to London where he produced *Judith* (1733) and *Joseph* (1745). If such as he did not play Kerl's works, what *did* they play?

The date of the publication of Muffat's *Componimenti Musicali* was until recently doubtful. 'Grove' gave 1727, Chrysander suggested *circa* 1735, but lately, after I had shown* that it must be after July, 1737, Herr Werner Wolffheim demonstrated—what had been suspected previously by Herr Guido Adler—that the year was 1739.† In fact probably not more than three or four months, if so many, intervened between the publication and Handel's use of it in *St. Cecilia's Day* (September, 1739). So it must have reached England almost at once. Theophilus Muffat (1690?—1770) was court-organist at Vienna, and *maestro di cembalo* of the Archduchesses and the Grand Duke of Tuscany. The Emperor accepted the dedication of the work, which appeared in handsome style. St. Cecilia is the prominent figure on the frontispiece. Now Muffat had certainly heard of Handel. There is extant a MS. dated 1736, in which he has adapted Handel's first book of suites and six fugues for the newer method of fingering, 'mises dans une autre applicature pour la facilité de la main par Théophile Muffat 1736.'‡ Moreover in the *Componimenti* he has displayed further knowledge. At the end of Handel's second book of suites, printed in 1733, and reprinted at Paris, 1736, stands a chaconne in G with 62 variations. And Muffat finishes his work too with a chaconne in G with 38 variations—on the same

---

* 'Z.I.M.G.,' Dec. 1907.

† 'Z.I.M.G.,' Feb. 1908.

‡ Herr Seiffert. 'S.I.M.G.,' i, 140.

ground bass, with some resemblance also of opening melody.

It was then from a work which pointedly challenged comparison with his own writings—we need not necessarily impute more than friendly rivalry—that Handel took themes or basses for his *St. Cecilia's Day* and for his grand concertos, published April, 1740. How was it that Handel acquired the work so early? It may have been so popular that it found its way to London music-sellers in two or three months. Or the exalted patronage accorded to it may have wafted it betimes to the English court, which had long been in close relations with that at Vienna. Or a copy may have been forwarded at once to Handel, whether by Muffat himself, or by some friend, either owing to its popularity or its emulation of Handel. But whatever alternative may appear the most probable, the idea of secrecy seems absolutely excluded. From Muffat himself Handel could never have wished to conceal his knowledge of the work. He must have noticed Muffat's acquaintanceship with his own suites, and yet he promptly sat down to write, and concurrently advertised the publication of 12 grand concertos in which there are a number of traces which could not possibly escape Muffat, or any one fairly familiar with the *Componimenti*. These concertos were specially advertised as issued with 'His Majesty's royal licence and protection.' They belonged to a class of work which was likely to circulate and to be reprinted abroad. We find a licence granted at Paris, May, 1739, for the printing of Handel's ' 5e 6e et 7e oeuvres.' * These concertos figure as Op. 6 in the English edition. Very possibly the continental and English numberings differed, though a licence for the concertos may have been taken out beforehand, as the issue of a set had been previously advertised, according to Burney. However this may have been, to Muffat those concertos

* M. Michel Brenet. 'S.I.M.G.,' viii, 439.

would probably make their way, so far as Handel could judge. And what would be the effect? Would it defend England from the irruption of copies of the *Componimenti?* On the contrary, it would cause the work to be the more talked of, and the more likely to circulate.

It is really inconceivable that Handel should have attempted to keep to himself his copy of the *Componimenti,* if he ever possessed one. And so far at least as *St. Cecilia's Day* is concerned, the common practices of the time do not seem to have been exceeded; at any rate it would be difficult to draw a clear distinction between the use of Muffat here, and Bach's use of *Almira.* And if it be said that a march in *Joshua* (1747) and a trio in *Theodora,* 1749, stand on a different footing, let us consider the likelihood of a man's keeping from his friends his knowledge of a brand-new work, which stood a good chance of reaching them in any case—he was contributing himself to that end by issuing the concertos—merely to be enabled to introduce some paltry, if improper borrowings 8 or 10 years later. And even then he unnecessarily writes ' Trio,' which might make identification easier. It will be agreed, I think, that all the circumstances make any idea of secrecy practically inadmissible, while on the other hand against an open recognition of Muffat's work by Handel there seems no objection to be urged.

We come next to the duets of the fourth composer. Giovanni Carlo Maria Clari is stated to have been born at Pisa, 1669, and to have died about 1745. A number of his works in MS. in the Fitzwilliam collection (Cambridge), including duets, masses, and a *Stabat Mater,* bear dates ranging from 1740 to 1753. If it be on the basis of these dates that ' Grove ' speaks of the duets as published, 1740—1747, and the interpretation be sound, the continuity of issue would imply a great popularity for these duets; and if the masses and *Stabat Mater* were also published, apparently after Clari's death, he must have been a very noted composer, and one from whom it would have been very unsafe to borrow secretly. But it must be confessed that this interpretation of the dates seems scarcely satisfactory. Is there a single copy extant of these many publications? Moreover, the dates in what is styled the first volume cover several years. Curiously enough, too, some of the duets, including the first two, bear no date; yet they cannot be supposed to have been all published singly.

It might be suggested that perhaps the dates mean the dates of the English copies, made by English scribes. If so, the duets used in *Theodora* were known in England by 1740. Yet there is a difficulty here, too; nobody is likely to have copied the duets in such small detachments over a period of seven years. The third alternative is to regard them as dates of composition. This perfectly satisfies the MS. phenomena, as a composer would not necessarily date each composition. Still it conflicts with Burney's statement that Clari's duets had circulated in manuscript long before their publication in 1720;* besides it is difficult to believe in a man born in 1669 being so fertile up to 1753, especially if he died about 1745.

There is a possible solution which may be suggested with great diffidence. Suppose this duet composer was not the Clari of Pisa born in 1669, but some later Clari, perhaps a son or grandson. The style of the duets, it has often been noticed, is more frequently associated with a comparatively late date. In a list of violinists of the early part of the 18th century, given by Burney (iii, 559) I find the name of Costantino Clari, also of Pisa, a writer of vocal duets and trios. How if the personalities and production of two writers of duets have been confused? If so, the dates may really have their usual

* *Hist.*, iii, 536.

significance.   The three volumes, two of duets and one of
trios, might have reached England together about 1748-49.

That *some* duets had, in fact, reached England about
that period is proved by two MSS. in the Fitzwilliam
collection.   These contain undated duets and trios by
Clari, entirely different from the above-mentioned three
volumes.   Both MSS. were copied by J. Burton, and one
bears the signature, J. Burton, March, 1752.   So that
some duets by some Clari were known in England during
Handel's lifetime and it is consonant with probabilities to
suppose the particular duets were also accessible when
Handel wrote *Theodora*.   Some, in fact, were printed in
England a few years later.   Clari's duets ranked traditionally next to Steffani's, the principal collection of which
was in the possession of Frederick, Prince of Wales.

Habermann, the last on the list, has earned no place in
'Grove' or 'Riemann,' and it might be thought that
Handel, during a visit to Germany in 1750, had picked up
the work of some obscure musician.   But Habermann had
once been in the service of the Grand Duke of Tuscany
at Florence; in 1743, he had the honour of composing an
opera to celebrate the coronation of Maria Theresa at
Prague;* and his pupils, we are told, were chiefly noble
and wealthy amateurs at Prague, though Dussek also was
amongst his scholars.   His masses (Op. 1) were published
in 1747.†   Now the great grandee of Prague was that
extremely enthusiastic young amateur, Prince Lobkowitz.
This prince, we find, came to England with Gluck at
the end of 1745, and remained about two years here,
devoting himself to music.‡   We may most naturally
view Handel's acquaintanceship with the masses as connected with Prince Lobkowitz.   In any case Handel must

* Mr. J. S. Shedlock. 'Mus. Times.'

† By a slip Mr. Sedley Taylor, p. 178, speaks of these as unpublished,
though he had given the date of publication on p. 15.

‡ 'Grove,' s. v. Lobkowitz.

surely have reflected that the Prince might return at any time. From Mrs. Delany's letters we gather that he was believed to be a suitor for the hand of an English lady.

The ' secrecy theory,' let us remind ourselves, will, or would, have it, that Handel ran the risks not in one case only but in all cases, and that without exception success crowned his enterprise. That he had no sufficient inducement to conceive the design is generally conceded; and those readers, whose patience has carried them through the preceding pages, will have set him down, I think, as the clumsiest and most injudicious plotter that history has to show. It might be, no doubt, that from a sense of humour, or as the result of some wager, he wished to prove how easily musicians in England and elsewhere might be hoodwinked; still the joke was not brief, and the wagering must have been often renewed. And all such theories are obliged to assume, without offering a scintilla of evidence, that a vast number of possible, even apparently likely, occurrences unanimously and with one consent refused to occur. They made quite a point of it. There was nothing unlikely, for instance, in Graun, who was a celebrated singer, whose death, in fact, was more deplored by Frederick the Great in his capacity of singer than in his rôle of composer,* being engaged at Hanover to entertain the English court May—October, 1735, especially as, owing to the deaths of two dukes at Brunswick, March 1st and September 3rd, that year, there could have been no great festivities in that town; nor in a *Passion* of his being introduced to the notice of the same court at Hanover, or at Brunswick. There is nothing unlikely in Handel's having merely borrowed the *Passion* MS.; indeed I should have thought that the order of the extracts, and the fact that no suggestion seems to be made of any trace of the use of Graun's work except from these

---

* Burney.

extracts, which must have been all made about 1736, furnish *prima facie* evidence that the MS. was only lent to Handel. I confess to a suspicion that the theorists have never been able to spare time to study the details; nor was this unnatural, for these details required some collecting. I had myself quite an open mind, until I had covered a good deal of ground in the examination.

CHAPTER XI.

POSSIBLE REASONS.

THROUGH the examination of individual cases, then, the 'secrecy' theory loses all its allurements. And here let me be allowed to enter a *caveat* against a prevalent impression that error, if it only imputes something unfavourable, enjoys an intellectual respectability which would be wanting to an error in the opposite direction. When the keeping to the straight line forms our ideal, why should a swerve to the right be less intelligent than a swerve to the left? Why should an excess in panegyric be a sign of greater mental weakness than an excess in depreciation? I would suggest that they are equally pardonable and equally estimable, and that your most respectable theory is that which accords best with the *data*.

If anyone still finds it a little strange that no petty-minded foe tried to make capital out of the circumstances, there can be no objection to supposing that such foes never fully realised the frequency or nature of the borrowings; their knowledge was not likely to be first-hand, and report would only reach them in some vague form such as 'taken from'; the man who heard of Graun might not hear of Muffat, the man who heard of Clari might not hear of Habermann. Each would be living his own life, of which his relation to Handel was a very small fragment.

It is a matter of curiosity merely to speculate *why* Handel preferred to borrow. No one reason is at all likely to cover all cases; in things indifferent we act from mixed and constantly varying motives. In the end we shall not be able to dispense entirely with the famous fifth reason for drinking: 'or any other reason why.' Monsieur Pirro endorses Spitta's suggestion about Bach's borrowings, that the Leipsic cantor desired to show his appreciation of other composers. Assuredly a recognition by Handel had no less value, and the cases of Cesti, Corelli, Mattheson, and Steffani, mentioned above, may have originated in such a feeling. To associate his honoured friend Steffani with the praise of music in *Solomon* was an idea that cast no reflection on Handel's sense of fitness. A quotation again from the *péripétie* of Carissimi's *Jephtha* at a corresponding place in *Alexander's Feast,* January, 1736, may be reasonably regarded as an identification of Carissimi, the father of oratorio, with Timotheus. And had Handel desired a representative of St. Cecilia in the same work, what better choice could he have made than Graun, the writer of a modern *Oratorium Passionale?* It may be accident, but a fugue theme adapted from Graun certainly does stand in the right place, ' with nature's mother wit, and arts unknown before.' The case of Muffat and *St. Cecilia's Day* has been noted above.

Only a very hasty thinker will expect one explanation to cover all cases. A desire to display skill in treatment, or an artistic impulse, as Dr. Chrysander suggested, making it seem a pity not to develop latent possibilities, occasionally perhaps lack of time; these, and other reasons may have operated. The desire to please powerful patrons should not be overlooked. The compositions of Graun, Muffat, Clari, and Habermann, seem well-fitted to please royal or noble amateurs, and by such the works may have been brought under Handel's notice. To his patrons he had to pay a certain amount of deference; he had to listen patiently to Jennens' strictures on *The Messiah;* when George II. condescended to arrange a programme, his wishes must be carried out; and we know that the suggestion of *Judas Maccabaeus* came from the Prince of Wales. It is quite possible that the Prince or the Princess Augusta, or both, were known to be admirers of Graun; if so, the appearance of the chorus in their *Wedding Anthem,* and its subsequent transference with another to *Il Trionfo,* a work advertised as 'by command of the Prince and Princess,'' is not calculated to astonish. It must have been of vital importance to Handel to disarm the hostility of the Prince, for the health of George II. in 1736 gave cause for anxiety. As observed above, in this year the Prince did discontinue his hostility.

With the exception of the 'Kerl,' which would be known at the Academy, the works might be well-known and admired in court circles, and Handel may have thought it judicious to introduce quotations. 'In the anonymous Demofoonte . . . the first air is an imitation of Handel's minuet in Ariadne . . . . These cookeries are generally intended to flatter Handel's admirers; but they never succeed.' Burney, *Hist.,* iv, 466. Handel also was not above the necessity of pleasing. Whether the works were performed in England cannot be decided, for our knowledge of the court and private concerts amounts to almost nothing. In Mrs. Delany's letters there is mention of a *Stabat Mater* (composer not named) performed at the Primate's house in Ireland. There may have been many such performances. Handel, we know, wrote a number of duets of which Mainwaring and the historians knew nothing, between 1740 and 1745; these must have been written for performance, and there is no reason why Clari's duets should not have been sung in the same circles. Of the 1716 *Passion* biographers and historians knew nothing; yet there seems little doubt that it was written and performed in England.* Perhaps Graun's *Passion* was similarly performed at Easter, 1736. Muffat's *Componimenti* may have been included in the répertoire of the Princesses; they must have played something besides Handel's suites.

If it were desired to illustrate further the possible

---

* See note B, p. 202.

varieties of reasons, it might be suggested that Handel adapted Kerl's canzona as a sort of chorale. *Israel* with its narrator has of all the oratorios the strongest resemblance to the *Passion* form. The same explanation might serve for the use of Lotti's *Miserere* in *The Triumph of Time*. For this chorus was merely transferred from the *Foundling Anthem*—a point not noticed by Mr. Sedley Taylor—and it is there neighboured by another which introduced (though without acknowledgment) the chorale 'Aus tiefer Noth.' In truth both quotations are perfectly apposite in the anthem.

However, speculations like these can put forward no claim to certainty. Their varying plausibilities cannot affect the firm conclusion that the borrowings were quite open. Beside this all else is of minor interest.

CHAPTER XII.

The Italian *MSS*.

The previous chapters have left on one side the *Magnificat* claimed by some to be the work of a priest called Erba, the *Te Deum* ascribed by Chrysander to Padre F. A. Urio (*circa* 1700), and the Serenata which bears the name of Alessandro Stradella.* That nothing whatever has been lost by taking this course will be clear on the slightest reflection. For whatever may have been Handel's relation to these compositions, their existence could not by one iota affect prejudicially the circulation of Muffat, Clari, Graun, or Habermann. Nor will it be seriously contended that Handel argued on this wise : ' I may with perfect safety make use of this old *Magnificat,* which no one in England has ever seen, or is ever likely to see; therefore I may with equal safety make use of these *Componimenti,* just come piping hot from Vienna with their deliberate emulation of myself.' However stoutly it be maintained that these were Italian works used in secret, still the withers of Clari and Muffat will remain unwrung; to these three works they would pay absolutely no manner of heed. It might be possible to demonstrate, if we may indulge in illustration, that the Duke of Wellington rode unrecognised through three or, if you will, ten thousand Little Peddlingtons, but this would not by one single inch advance the theory that on a number of occasions he rode quite unrecognised down Piccadilly. Or take another illustration. Supposing that a man is in the grip of seven deadly diseases at once, you will scarcely raise his spirits by assuring him you can diagnose in addition three ailments, from which, in your

---

* For the use of these works " Grove's Dictionary " may be consulted.

judgment, he may really with fair luck hope to escape alive.

The other compositions were used, so far as can be judged, when they were enjoying to the full such vogue as ever fell to their lot. But there is not the slightest ground for believing that these three ever had a vogue at all; indeed there is not a shred of evidence that they were ever seen by any man but Handel until after his death. By no process of reason—and processes of unreason we shall not intentionally use—can any relation be established between these three and the other group. It cannot be argued that because Handel made use of Kerl or Haber-mann, all copyists, into whose hands these three might fall, became in consequence immune from error. It cannot even be argued that because Handel thought proper to make use of Graun, or Clari, he would therefore think it equally proper to make use of Erba, or Stradella. He might, perhaps, or he might not; but there is absolutely nothing to guide us to a conclusion.

These three works, standing apart, living as it were in a different hemisphere, or with sun and stars of their own, possess an interest of a very high order. Perhaps the most obviously interesting is the 'Urio' *Te Deum,* which seems most eminently calculated to excite curiosity. The feeling of standing in the presence of something elvish, something 'not altogether of this world,' may pardonably steal over those who shall chance to compare the headings on the manuscripts with the elucidations supplied by Dr. Chry-sander. This *Te Deum,* we collect, was the offspring of a 'Cerberus, three gentlemen at once'; it was sired by one 'Urio—a Jesuit of Bologna'; also by a Padre Frañco Uria [*sic*] Bolognese ; also by F. A. Urio, not of Bologna, but of Milan (Chrysander). Its births, moreover, would seem to have exceeded the births of Bacchus; it was born first of all in 1660; again *apud* 1682; and again, with ardour undiminished, *circa* 1700 (Chrysander). Such a bantling, with its history so weird, so Pythagorean, 'gives furiously to think,' I should imagine. At any rate it can well make room for yet a fourth appearance on this world's stage, but now under the auspices of Handel *circa* May 18, 1709. And I hope to give sufficient reason for assigning births to the 'Erba' and 'Stradella,' very similar to this fourth 'Urio' appearance.

The recognition of Handel's authorship will be equally welcomed, I would fain hope, by all schools of thought. For though it may not be altogether impossible to believe, with Dr. Chrysander, that Handel's use of these works also was known to his contemporaries, still the peculiarly extensive use of the 'Erba' in *Israel,* and the use of the 'Urio' for a work of the same nature, the *Dettingen Te Deum,* which was annually performed in St. Paul's Cathedral, might fairly have been expected to leave public traces. We really *should* have expected the tradition about the 'Erba,' known *ex hypothesi* to the Academy of Antient Musick, to have survived the ravages of time. We really *should* have expected the tradition about the 'Urio,' annually refreshed as it would be, to find a place in the pages of the historians. And we should have expected it equally, whether the works came to England with full publicity about 1738, or whether, as I hope to show, they came with Handel from Italy about 1709. In the latter case Handel would presumably bring them away because of their merits, and to these merits he would naturally direct the attention of English musicians, in particular to Stradella's, for his compositions were highly esteemed. Yet Burney, who hunted diligently after Stradella's works, knew nothing of this. I do not contend that these are fatal objections; but a difficulty, a very considerable difficulty, they do seem to create.

The opposite theory, again, wears a braver appearance, when these works are struck off the list. For, if conceived to have come to England about 1738, why were the manuscripts taken (by night ?) to Handel, who was not a collector, and deeply in debt, rather than to some rich collector of music? And supposing it agreed that Handel brought them out of Italy in 1709, presumably on account of their merits, is it likely that he should have kept them hidden, with the far-sighted design of making improper use of them some thirty years later? This is surely to impute a length of vision greater than should be credited to ordinary mortals. The *Te Deum* should have interested English musicians, for a *Te Deum* on that large scale by an Italian was a thing such as they could never have met with before. And the Serenata, if by Stradella, should have been an object of the greatest interest. Stradella's reputation stood high in England; Purcell is said to have deeply lamented his death; and yet, beyond solo cantatas, we do not seem to hear of his works having reached England. And a little after Handel's settling down in England, the interest in Stradella would be quickened by the romantic account of him given in Bonnet-Bourdelot's *Histoire de la Musique et de ses effets* (Paris, 1715).

According to this story Stradella eloped with a lady from Venice to Rome, and assassins were despatched to the Eternal City, who tracked him down, and waited to kill him, when he should emerge from the church of St. John in Laterano. And as they waited, to their ears floated forth, from inside the church, the wondrous strains of *San Giovanni Battista,* the oratorio which Stradella had just composed. In an agony of contrition they revealed to Stradella what had been their fell purpose, and conjured him to fly. To Turin, therefore, he fled with the lady, Hortensia, but even here he was not secure. His implacable enemies discovered him, and made a murderous yet not quite fatal attack. His wounds being healed, he fled with Hortensia to Genoa, and here at last, within a year, the daggers of the assassins were plunged into the hearts of both. Something in this way runs the tale of Bonnet-Bourdelot, which obtained wide credence, and seems to

have really had a considerable groundwork of truth.* In
England it was examined and accepted in the main by
Wanley, a careful writer, who died in 1726. A tale like
this was bound to be discussed, wherever musicians in
England gathered together, and are we to conceive of
Handel as sitting silent, and giving no hint of the treasure,
as his fellows would have deemed it, lying in his library,
or in his iron-bound trunks?

These objections again are not urged as being fatal, but
as being incumbrances to a general theory; without them
its path would be smoothed to a certain extent. For this
reason the following discussion may gain a little in interest.
Unfortunately it cannot avoid a little complexity; it
cannot escape entering into minutiae; it cannot free itself
from ramifications. The reader will not be invited to
witness a brilliant *coup de main* or two; it is patient sap-
ping and mining that court his attention. Some main
features, however, when envisaged as a whole, seem to me
sufficiently striking, and I have thought best to prefix a
slight sketch, taking a personal form, which shall exhibit
some of the chief outlines, disencumbered of small details.
Those who have read this sketch will then be better placed
for grasping those larger positions, to which the more
detailed discussions are ancillary. I also endeavour to
show that some objections which might possibly be urged
beforehand, have no real weight; and I recall to the reader's
mind some of the general principles, which apply to
inquiries such as this. It is only after these preliminaries
that the more complete treatment commences.

* Heinz Hess, *Die Opern Alessandro Stradellas*, 1906, casts new light on
Stradella, superseding all other accounts.

CHAPTER XIII.

First Sketch.

Some three years ago while turning over Mr. Abdy Williams' very useful 'Life of Handel,' I chanced upon a passage which puzzled me for a brief space of time. The text quoted some words written on the last page of *La Resurrezione,* an oratorio commonly ascribed to Handel. The words ran: 'Roma la Festa di Pasque dal Marchese Ruspoli 11 d'Aprile 1708.' How now! was my thought; was this oratorio really written by the (dal) Marchese Ruspoli? Fortunately Mr. Williams strangled this bewilderment at its birth. 'Dal' means here 'at the house of,' a usage well-recognised and ancient, but quite uncommon on manuscripts. The words simply mean that Handel wrote the work while staying 'at the house of' the Marquis Ruspoli.

Now this somehow reminded me of a *Magnificat* that Monsieur Victor Schoelcher thought was also written at Rome, and of a controversy as to the meaning of a 'del' on one MS. of this work, which bears a heading 'Del R^d Sig^r Erba.' And with this before the mind, even Sherlock Holmes' medical friend himself could not have missed observing, how easily a similar note at the back of the original MS. of the *Magnificat,* running '. . . . . . . dal R^d Sig^r Erba . . . ,' might also have been mistaken (or misread) by an English copyist. Perhaps ninety-nine out of a hundred would interpret it as implying authorship; but, of course, when reproducing it, the copyist would use the word which meant the same as 'dal' (as he would think), viz., 'del,' which was beyond comparison the more usual and is indeed the more correct form. Here, then, was revealed a very plain way in which a blunder *might* have occurred; Handel *might* have stayed at the house of some priest called Erba.*

It occurred to me to wonder whether the manuscripts of that other rather mysterious work, ascribed to some Urio, might be susceptible of a similar explanation. I therefore consulted ' Grove's Dictionary ' s.v. Urio, and saw very quickly that these copyists were quite guiltless of such a blunder. Yet I happened to compare, a little idly, the different headings, and observed that, if ordinary critical principles held (and why should they not so hold ?), the headings sprang from an original ' Te Deum   Urio.'

As the reader will suppose, this bare ' Urio ' did not fill me with absolute confidence in Urio as the composer. The word might mean many things; it might have originated in a hundred ways. Was Urio a common name, I wondered; but in any case I had no Italian directory at hand. Yet, if common, it might also be found in an atlas. I took down the nearest atlas, one of Keith Johnston's,† found in the map of Switzerland the Italian village Urio, lying 5 to 6 miles north of Como, and the very next name that caught my eye, 10 miles E. of Como, was Erba! No man, of woman born, could have escaped the wild idea, that Handel might have been in the district, and written works at these places.‡ The accounts of his Italian wanderings admitted of such a stay in the spring or summer

---

* To avoid mistakes, let me say at once that I agree entirely with Dr. Chrysander and Mr. Sedley Taylor in their interpretation of ' del.' The copyist must unquestionably be supposed to have regarded some Erba as the composer. But that does not take us far. The real question is what was on the original MS. from which he made his copy; whether *there* stood a 'del', or not rather a 'dal' similar to that on the MS. of *La Resurrezione*. For a fuller account of the note on this MS. see p. 181.

† Had I happened to consult an atlas by any other cartographer, I might never have pursued the subject.

‡ Though still regarding this as a possible explanation of the 'Erba,' as well as of the 'Urio,' I prefer for the 'Erba' the original suggestion about 'dal.' The ways of error are numberless, and we cannot be sure.

of 1709; this date would remove all alleged objections on the score of Italianisation of style; moreover, there was then an opportunity for the writing of a *Te Deum,* owing to the universal expectation of an European peace in May of that year.

Before making this last observation I had sent a letter to the ' Musical Times ' (Dec., 1905), hoping that some one might be able to follow up the suggestion. I had not been able to examine the ' Urio ' *Te Deum* in Dr. Watson's Manchester library, as the book had been temporarily mislaid; but I happened to turn over the pages of the ' Stradella ' serenata, which had also been used in *Israel,* and noticed that the third movement of the Overture (or Sinfonia) had probably given the suggestion for the duet 'Happy we' (*Acis and Galatea, circa* 1720), so that Handel owed another idea to Stradella. The fugue-like subject of the second movement of this overture also reminded me vaguely and dimly of something, which gradually identified itself with the theme of ' Retrieve the Hebrew name ' (*Saul*); but that, I knew, was really derived from the ' Urio '! Now this observation was made without the slightest *arrière pensée*. I had no more thought of this inspection of the one fugal subject of the ' Stradella ' leading me to the ' Urio,' than of its leading me to the Choral symphony or to the Malay Archipelago.

And here let us pause for a moment to consider what we know of Handel. We know that he was very fond of treating old ideas afresh, a leaning perhaps analogous to the love of ' variations ' in later composers, and that often the resemblance between the new and the old is extremely slight. For instance, the air ' Where shall I seek ' (*Acis*) must unquestionably have been suggested by an air in his second *Passion* (*circa* 1716), in spite of the triviality of the resemblance, because several other movements in *Acis* sprang from the same *Passion,* one chorus with little alteration. And again, like other minds, Handel's mind worked by association of ideas; one idea would suggest another with which it had some bond of connexion; he would not jump suddenly from China to Patagonia, but rather from China to Japan. Think of Thackeray's *Vanity Fair* at 10 o'clock, and at 10.1 you are more likely to be thinking of *The Newcomes* than of Dante's *Divina Commedia,* or of Kant's *Critique of Pure Reason.* And if, unexpectedly, one minute past ten does find you thinking of Dante, that is probably because Thackeray has been somehow associated in your mind with Dante on some previous occasion. I shall try to exhibit what has all the appearance of being the working of Handel's mind in different compositions, including amongst others the 'Urio' and the 'Stradella.' And when we are confronted with such appearances, it is surely more intelligent to attribute them to such mental working, than to invoke the blind goddess of Chance at every turn. Not long ago I passed by a street in a new neighbourhood, displaying the name ' Patey St.' The intersecting street which I first noticed was 'Santley St.' Rash though it may have been, I really could not repress the suspicion, that the man who named those streets was not altogether unacquainted with English music. Whether the succeeding names, Tallis, Purcell, Barnby, Parratt, Prout, confirmed or annihilated the theory, I shall leave to the judgment of the reader. For my part, when facing a stately pile like that of Drury Lane Theatre, I shall always prefer to attribute its origin to the mind of some architect, rather than to conceive it (on the authority of copyists) rising casually through ' casual mortar ' encountering ' casual lime.'

To resume. When, shortly afterwards, the 'Urio' *Te Deum* was rediscovered, I found, to my surprise, that the ' Happy we' little theme (*Acis*) showed its face also in the ' Urio.' And again between duets for canto and basso in each work there was quite a striking resemblance. I felt now as sure as need be that the ' Urio ' had borrowed from the 'Stradella.' A later work may be allowed one accidental resemblance to an earlier, I think, just as a dog is allowed his first bite; at a pinch, perhaps, even two might pass; but three are really too many. And I could discover no objection whatever to the natural inference that Handel must have written the *Te Deum.*

It was, of course, worth while to cast about for fresh evidence, and the obvious thought was: 'If Handel wrote it, he might have used ideas also from his own earlier works.' Unfortunately works written in Italy would prove nothing, as it could always be argued, that at the very first inn, at which he stayed in Italy, he found this *Te Deum* stowed away in a worm-eaten chest in some disused loft. And of the larger Hamburg compositions only two were extant, so that the chances of finding anything seemed rather slender. However, I examined first the opera *Almira,* and discovered nothing. Then I tried the early (1704) *Passion,* and here I found, not indeed *other* ideas, but apparently earlier and duller versions of the *same two themes,* which had first attracted my attention, and, like the 'Stradella' forms, they were in *consecutive movements.* Without doubt, this was remarkable. It was not that the resemblances, taken separately, were so very rich and rare (though stronger than not a few on the ground of which, though standing alone, Handel has been credited with borrowing); the wonder was how, like the fly in amber, they ever got there at all. However, I proceeded, and noted, now with a *blasé* feeling, that there was no ' accident' about a very slight resemblance which I had previously observed between the ' Urio' fugue-theme and that of a second ' Urio' chorus, *standing next* to our ' Happy we ' theme. This second theme was clearly made up of the rudiments of the *Passion* fugue theme, and the counterpoint which follows as a continuation in this *Passion* movement. In fact in later entries the *Passion* theme is found with little modification. *So that in each of these three works we find the resemblances in consecutive movements.*

Yet this is not all. There is only one fugal movement in the fourth work, *Acis*; what would have been the chances against this movement standing next after 'Happy we' (in the original version), of its having a theme of a similar character to our previous fugue-theme, and of its exhibiting a very unusual structure, to which I have found no parallel in Handel's works except the corresponding above-mentioned chorus—they are both in five parts—in the 'Urio' *Te Deum?* Yet so it is, another wild improbability, on the 'accident' hypothesis, has materialised.

I had thus traced, apparently, two themes, found side by side in the *Passion,* through the 'Stradella' and 'Urio,' in each of which they appeared side by side, till they emerged in *Acis,* the fugue theme hardly recognisable. The original of the 'Happy we' theme would thus be the second air of the crucifixion section of the 1704 *Passion.* Was Handel, I wonder, led to think of this air when writing *Acis,* by the fact that the air 'As when the dove,' immediately preceding 'Happy we,' was by universal consent derived from the *second air in the crucifixion section* of his 1716 *Passion?* There is another odd thing too. Of our *Acis* fugal chorus, 'Wretched lovers,' the second section, 'Behold the monster Polypheme,' *may* certainly have been suggested by a duet 'No more barbarous rage and horrid din'—words distinctly Polyphemic—in the Italian cantata *Io languisco;* and to this cantata, before noticing the resemblance, I had assigned an origin contemporaneous with that of the 'Urio' *Te Deum;* it also seems to have been written in expectation of the same European peace.*

A word of explanation is necessary here. This chorus 'Behold the monster Polypheme' it might be said, was notoriously adapted from a movement in the Hanover duet *Caro Autor.* That is perfectly true. But observe that in a later

* See note C, p 204.

version of this duet *Caro Autor*, for the above movement another was substituted, derived, as Chrysander (i, 361) has pointed out, from the duet 'Per abbatter' in the Italian cantata *Fillide e Aminta*. But this duet 'Per abbatter' was, as he has also pointed out in his edition, transferred almost note for note to the above cantata *Io languisco* with the words mentioned above, 'Non più barbaro furore, etc.' And inspection shows that this form is merely an earlier version of the Hanover duet movement; this would be proved by the resemblance, even apart from Handel's action in the substitution. Just as we seem to find 'Happy we' *suggested* by the *Passion* air, and yet with more resemblance to the later 'Urio' duet, so here Handel's mind might first turn to the cantata *Io languisco*, though he would actually depend more on the form assumed by the duet a few years later.

Here then has been displayed a very curious sequence, which the most devoted worshipper of Chance will refuse, I think, to set down entirely to accident. He will prefer to admit the derivations of the *Acis* movements, at least, all the more readily because, as he might acutely and justly point out, this does not necessarily involve the dependence of the 'Urio' and 'Stradella' on the *Passion*. It merely proves, he might say, that *Acis* borrowed from the 'Urio.' Nevertheless if successive steps have led to a true conclusion, these steps must themselves deserve very careful examination. And it will appear later, I think, that the resemblances between the *Passion,* 'Urio' and 'Stradella,' are, humanly speaking, beyond the power of accident. This in effect will prove Handel's authorship of the 'Urio.' And this again will afford us an elevation from which alleged *a priori* improbabilities in the other cases, particularly that of style, may be more accurately estimated. It may be found convenient now to glance at these supposed improbabilities.

CHAPTER XIV.

TRIFLING OBJECTIONS.

(1) *Handel undoubtedly borrowed from Muffat, etc.; therefore, etc.* It would be unkind to drag this argument from its Cimmerian gloom. Let us cast our eyes rather on the far more frequent borrowings from Handel's own early works. In doubtful cases the presumption takes the side of the stronger battalions; arithmetic, the most impartial of judges, rejects the argument with contempt.

(2) *It is not likely that three MSS. used in Israel should have gained wrong ascriptions.* Answer: (*a*) In any case this could form no objection to one or two of the works being Handel's. (*b*) In the case of the 'Urio,' the MSS. allow us to see it occurring, so that the number really is reduced to two; for it is a recognised principle that when the issue of part of a whole is known, you must make your calculations afresh. It was seven to one against a penny turning up 'heads' three times running. But the first spin has proved 'heads.' It is now only three to one against success. (*c*) The special circumstances here might easily lead to blunders. These MSS. (all or two of them), having been used in the same work, and dating from about the same period, might naturally have reposed side by side in Handel's library. A single misapprehension, then, might result in their leaving the library together, accompanied by the impression that, whoever might be the composer of each, it was certainly not Handel. All the same, having belonged to Handel they would enjoy a special interest; their possessors would *wish* to have the name of a definite composer attached; and such wishes partake of the nature of prophecies; they tend to produce their own fulfilment.

(3) *But would not Smith, jun., who inherited all Handel's musical MSS., prevent mistakes?* (a) Smith's close connexion with the composer only began when Handel was aged and half blind. In a thousand ways it is clear that Smith did not cross-question him about bygone years. Towards the end of his life Handel, never a great talker, was particularly silent and uncommunicative. And a great part of what Smith happened to hear would be completely forgotten, before he parted with the MSS. (b) But there is not the slightest reason for supposing Smith had any connexion with the mistakes. In 1774 he retired to Bath, having left all his MSS., it is stated, to the king. To London he never returned; he refused even the king's personal request, that he should be present at the Handel Commemoration in 1784; he felt that at his advanced age the strain and excitement would be too much for him. (c) All the MSS., we are told, were left to the king, and yet they are by no means all to be found at Buckingham Palace; the collection is scattered, and scattered in such a way as to indicate great carelessness or ignorance in those responsible. Parts of the original scores of *Rinaldo, Ottone,* and many another work, are lodged in the Fitzwilliam collection. The arranger must have approached his task with a light heart.

(4) *But the biographers say nothing about a stay near Lake Como, nor of an acquaintance called Erba.* This argument will not appeal to those who have read Mainwaring's *Life.* He mentions very few Italian friends or patrons. He says nothing of the Marchese Ruspoli, who seems nevertheless to have been Handel's principal patron at Rome. He is silent about Cardinal Grimani, who wrote the libretto of *Agrippina,* and was Austrian Viceroy at Naples during Handel's stay there. He extends Handel's stay in Italy to six years, though it could scarcely have been four, and probably was under three, while his account of still earlier years is a tissue of absurdities. (b)

At the same time his account would carry great weight in the years 1770—1780. In spite of its untrustworthiness it would still be the only authority, and its catalogue might well seem complete, and acquire almost the dignity of a canon. Yet it omits the oratorio *La Resurrezione,* the three Roman psalms (1707), the *Salve Regina* and *Silete venti,* and indeed all sacred works written in Italy. Both *Passions* are absent. The early opera *Silla* is also missing, which is significant in view of what is mentioned under the next heading. Of the Italian serenatas only *Il Trionfo* and *Aci* are mentioned by name.

(5) *But it is not likely that Handel's powerful name should have been displaced* [Grove, s.v. Erba]. (a) Now even for this there happens to be one instructive precedent. In Eitner's *Quellen Lexicon* there are entered some *viola da gamba* sonatas as the work of Leffloth of Nüremberg. Herr A. Einstein, feeling an interest, inquired for the MS. at the place named by Eitner, but discovered to his surprise that the MS. contained Handel's sonatas for *viola da gamba.* The copy had been made by Graupner in 1739; he should have known the truth, and yet the name of Leffloth is certainly on the manuscript. Inspection solved the puzzle; Handel's name had been coolly crossed out, and Leffloth's substituted. These sonatas are very juvenile productions of Handel's, and Herr Einstein* conjectures that the eraser, sagaciously observing differences in style as compared with other works, cast about for a more likely composer, and fixed on Leffloth, who happened to have written works with some similarity of form. ' I think I see them at their work—these sapient trouble-tombs.' (b) But no necessity whatever would compel the MSS. to bear Handel's name. Of anonymous MSS. there exist hordes untold. According to ' Grove' there are 3,492 manuscripts in the Christ Church collection, and of these 1,075 bear no composer's name. Neither the score of *Almira* nor the

---

* 'S.I.M.G.,' iv, 170.

score of the *Passion,* the only two survivors of Handel's large Hamburg compositions, bears his or any other name. And what are we to make of that MS. in the British Museum, ' Silla, an opera by Gio. Bononcino,' once in the possession of Sir John Hawkins? Beyond all possible dispute this opera was written by Handel, whose autograph has been preserved in part. This MS., or the MS. from which it was transcribed, must have borne no name originally, so invention was called into play.* One cannot help wondering whether this *Silla* MS. was the victim of the same mistake as the ' Erba,' etc. As observed above, the opera is omitted from Mainwaring's catalogue.

(6) *But does not style form an objection to Handelian authorship?* We are dealing here merely with *a priori* objections. It will be sufficient, therefore, to remark: (*a*) Handelian authorship of the *Magnificat* was never doubted till the ' Erba ' MS. emerged, and Sir George Macfarren and Mr. W. S. Rockstro judged the work Handel's on the ground of style. (*b*) Professor Prout (' Monthly Musical Record,' Nov., 1871), who was certainly not then advocating Handel's claims, wrote these words with regard to the ' Urio ':—' The following air, " Tibi omnes Angeli," though exactly in Handel's manner throughout, has not been appropriated bodily like the preceding chorus.' (*c*) The same writer (Dec., 1871), discussing the ' Stradella,' observes : ' . . . the lady from the house sings a recitative and air very Handelian in style.' (*d*) If anyone has attempted to show that the works are exactly in the manners of Erba, Urio, and Stradella respectively, I have been unfortunate in never hearing of his essay.

* There is at Buckingham Palace a manuscript bearing Handel's name, on which appears a note, signed F. Chrysander, suggesting Telemann as the composer. If Handel was not the author, then his name is the fruit of some man's conjecture ; suppose him the composer, and how easily, had this note been affixed a hundred and thirty years ago, might we have had a copy with the lying title, ' del Signor G. P. Telemann.'

7) *But is it not strange that there should happen to have been composers named Urio and Erba living about the time when Handel was in Italy?* Here at last it is pleasant to be able to return a whole-hearted affirmative. Strange undoubtedly, almost as strange as there being two places, Urio and Erba, so close together in Italy. It is through these little ironies of life that problems arise. Something similar there is in the puzzle of the 'Iron Mask.' The pretensions of Count Matthioli seem quite unable to cope with the assaults of Monsieur Lair, Mr. Andrew Lang, and others, and yet the death of the 'Mask' actually was registered with the name of 'Marchialy.' There was, by the bye, a composer called Utrecht connected in some way with Hanover;* now Handel came from Hanover just before composing the 'Utrecht' *Te Deum.* I do not see how we can help falling victims frequently to these accidents; their false fires may be our only illumination. But when we can grasp something substantial, such things may be neglected.

* Herr T. Norlind, 'S.I.M.G. ix, 230.

CHAPTER XV.

CHANCE OR DESIGN.

THERE will be nothing novel about the principles described here. They are but common property, always at the service of him who desires them. But this being an age of advertisement, a little preliminary puff will do no harm.

The cogency of an argument, as it seems to me, is not in the slightest degree affected by the result to which it leads. If a certain strength of evidence is allowed to prove a borrowing, an equal or greater strength may surely prove a non-borrowing. Proof is not proof,

> ' Which alters when it alteration finds,
> Or bends with the remover to remove.'

Now it is on 'placing,' on juxtaposition, that the proof of a borrowing, strictly speaking, depends. It is not that each and every resembling phrase or bar, in a second writer, *might* not have occurred to him spontaneously. It is that the placing of the resembling bars or phrases in the same movement, and in more or less the same order, is, humanly speaking, beyond the range of accident. Let me illustrate by a passage from Sir Walter Scott, where the Antiquary, Jonathan Oldbuck, laments, on the sea-marge, the carrying-off of his beloved cane by the *phoca*, the doughty seal : ' I cut it in the classic woods of Haw-thornden when I did not expect always to have been a bachelor—I would not have given it for an ocean of seals.' Compare these words now with the outpouring of Shylock over the ring which Jessica had sold : ' I had it of Leah when I was a bachelor; I would not have given it for a wilderness of monkeys.' Every one, I think, will agree that this is an unacknowledged borrowing by the Antiquary, yet how trivial the resemblances! It is the combination, the juxtaposition, which forbids us to doubt.

Again, it is a recognised principle that two themes, each occurring in two works, have immeasurably greater force in proving a borrowing than a single theme of equal importance.* But it is not so commonly realised that two resemblances between themes, say of six notes each in two works, are considerably less likely to be due to accident than a single resemblance of twelve notes. For in the latter case, when creating the second six notes, the minds of the two composers were fettered by the previous six notes— fettered in time-value and rhythm, and by aesthetic considerations. But when they were planning their second movements, there lay before them the whole range of musical possibility, and yet they took the same path.

The same principle, in a slightly different aspect, teaches us the folly of overlooking apparent trifles. Nowadays all recognise that a most remarkable facial resemblance constitutes a far less certain ground of identification, than is afforded by anthropological measurements, individually very inconclusive, and yet collectively overwhelming. In the *Mystery of Marie Roget,* E. A. Poe has expressed this principle in a popular form :—

> ' What, of itself, would be no evidence of identity, becomes, through its corroborative position, proof most sure. . . . But it is not that the corpse was found to have the features of the missing girl, or found to have her shoes or her bonnet, or the flowers of her bonnet, or her feet, or a peculiar mark upon the arm, or her general size and appearance—it is that the corpse had each and *all collectively.* Could it be proved that the editor of *L'Etoile really* entertained a doubt, under the circumstances, there would be no need in his case of a commission *de lunatico inquirendo.*

* With Sir George Grove, *Beethoven and his nine Symphonies,* p. 299, it seems to have been enough, if the second theme occurred *anywhere* in the works of the later composer.

For different minds the weight of evidence from resemblances differs. Some reminiscence-hunters will allow nothing for chance.* For others, in their good-nature, chance is all-powerful. I have tried to found calculations on actual experience, and have estimated the average resemblance of those, on which I rely, as occurring by chance once in ten times, when two works, each with 31 main themes, are compared So far as my experience goes, indeed, this figure (10) is really too low; compare, for instance, some works whose independence is practically certain, viz., Bach's four large extant choral works with Handel's twenty oratorios. This gives us eighty trials; yet I doubt whether there is a single real resemblance to be found. Assuredly the figure is ridiculously low, if judged by the practice of many highly-respected writers.

For the sake of simplicity, again, I have deviated a little from strict mathematics, yet always against myself. I have taken the average chance of accident in single-barrelled themes as $1/10$; the chances of two accidents in two movements as $1/100$; of three $1/1000$, though strictly the figures, in the second and third instances especially, should be higher. The works are of course not all of 31 main themes, but here again a strict mathematical adjustment would only increase the strength of the argument. The force of the resemblances occurring in consecutive movements is estimated in this way. The place of the first resemblance in each work is supposed fixed. Then the other theme in each work might be in anyone of 31-1, or 30 places. Its chance of being in any given place is $1/30$; its chance of either immediately preceding or immediately following the first movement is $2/30$, or $1/15$. The chance of the resemblances being consecutive in *each* work is therefore $1/15$ ×

---

* A striking instance is the derivation in 'Grove' (s. v. Handel) of the four-note theme of the above-mentioned ' Wretched lovers' (*Acis, circa* 1720) from Bach's W.T.C., 1722. Mr. Balfour (*Essays and Addresses*) has already pointed out the absurdity.

$^1/_{15}=^1/_{225}$. But the chance of two resemblances occurring at all is only $^1/_{10} \times ^1/_{10}=^1/_{100}$. So the total chance of two consecutive resemblances in two works taken at random is $^1/_{22500}$; that is, it would only occur on an average once in 22,500 trials. For convenience in future I shall write 10, 15, for $^1/_{10}$, $^1/_{15}$, etc. Let it be noted that this principle of multiplication in 'double events' is recognised not only by all mathematicians, but by those very practical people, the bookmakers at race-meetings.

As to slight resemblances in secondary phrases succeeding the first themes, I propose to regard them as occurring accidentally only once in ten times. I am conscious that such estimates are only approximate; personally I think the figure 10 here is too low; but I should be grateful to anyone who could give a more precise estimate. Nothing is really gained by a man who says airily ' Oh ! these things cannot be reduced to figures,' and hugs himself in his obscurantism. All arguments from resemblance, all tales of curious coincidence, imply figures, though the precise figures may not often be obtainable. A man in America writes his English sweetheart's name on a piece of wood, and throws it into the sea; after a time it is cast on the English shores, and is picked up, singularly enough, by the sweetheart herself. Now if every piece of wood found its way to the coast of England, and every such piece were examined, and the girl formed one of a million and one souls residing on the western coast, the chances against such an accident would be a million to one in any given case. But our surprise is the greater because 'only a few' would come ashore, and 'only a few' would be examined. That expression 'only a few' implies figures, but the experience to decide whether it means one in 10, one in 100, or one in 1000, is generally wanting.

But in many cases of curious coincidence the figures are by no means evasive. Among a number of alleged true cases of coincidence, given in a magazine article, one of the most wonderful is this. Three scholars of Balliol College, Oxford, in for the Ireland Scholarship in 1876, determined to try the *sortes* with a *Corpus Poetarum Latinorum*. The line which fate gave them was Claudian, *De Laudibus Stilichonis*, ii. 251 :—

> '. . . totam cum Scotus Iernen
> Movit,'

Ierne means Ireland, and the Scot (Scotus) 'moved' Ireland. Wonderful to relate, the Ireland scholarship *was* carried off that year by a Walter Scott. Casting no doubt on the scrupulous accuracy of the tale, we observe that the *Corpus* contains under 170,000 lines; and that, according to the University Calendar, Scott is the name of about one undergraduate in 500 on an average. So the chances against this happening at a given date were less than 170,000 × 500, or 85 million to one.

To the power of chance there is, strictly speaking, no mathematical limit; Kerl's canzona and Handel's chorus might be quite independent. But in practice the line must be drawn at some point, and the only question is where. When a stranger brings out dice, and throws sixes ten times running, only the most charitable retain their perfect confidence in his honour, despite his assertions that the dice are not loaded. To question the connexion of the *Passion*, 'Urio,' and 'Stradella,' seems to require a faith equally touching. Or let us give a 'cocked hat and dress-cane' to an occurrence in connexion with Graun and Handel. Professor Prout, after some interesting experiences, which are not relevant here—the real wonder is that the discovery had not been made previously—perceived that some pages in Handel's sketch-books were identical with a chorus from a *Passion* of Graun's, and, by a curious stroke of chance, a few minutes before making the discovery he had acquired a catalogue, which advertised for sale that very *Passion*. But let us be more romantic. Suppose that the very second at which, in the Fitzwilliam library, Cambridge, Professor Prout had said : 'That is Graun's *Passion,*' the bell had rung, a catalogue containing 2000 entries was delivered by the postman, the librarian quite at random opened the catalogue, and the very first entry that caught his eye was this *Passion* of Graun. Suppose that a catalogue containing the work would only reach Cambridge once in 100,000 years, and that the postman might deliver letters at any second in the day. What are the chances against this dramatic incident ?

$$100,000 \times 365 \times 24 \times 60 \times 60 \times 2000 = 6307,200000,000000.$$

George Washington might conceivably gain credence for such a tale ; but shall we believe a tale of equal or greater improbability, vouched for by copyists, whose evidence breaks down under examination ?

Let us take lastly a musical illustration. Dr. Chrysander accepted apparently (i, 347) as sufficiently proved—and I believe it is generally accepted—the derivation of Handel's 'Music spread' (*Solomon*), solo and chorus, from a two-part movement in a motet of Steffani. These are the points of resemblance ; the second sections do not follow at precisely the same intervals in the two works, but that is of no importance.

Observe the very considerable difference in the first phrases, and the slightness of resemblance in the second phrases, which are of different lengths. I do not see how the first part can be estimated at more than 10. For slight resemblances in subsidiary second and third phrases I have been content to estimate 10.* But these second phrases perhaps have a greater resemblance than our average. Let us put the figure at 600; that is, if 600 composers had to continue the first phrase, only one would produce something as like Steffani's as Handel's actual phrase. The total resemblance, then, might happen by accident once in $10 \times 600 = 6000$ times. Now among alleged borrowings of a minor order this fills quite a respectable position; evidence, therefore, a million million times stronger should be regarded as conclusive for practical purposes.

* P. 129.

CHAPTER XVI.

The Chain.

I.

The kind reader will probably keep in mind, that when an arch is being constructed to bear a certain weight, it is no fair criticism to point out the absurd inadequateness of each separate stone to accomplish anything whatsoever. The resemblances to be noted here are admittedly such as, taken separately, might each well be the result of chance; but the real question is whether chance can reasonably be made responsible for the whole series. I shall commence by exhibiting an apparent connexion, not contended for as certain as yet, but merely as worth bearing in mind, between the 'Urio,' the 'Stradella,' and a work written by Handel at Rome, July 13, 1707, the *Nisi Dominus,* called for short 'N. D.' Not only will this give valuable help to the main argument, but it will illustrate effectively the manner in which a theme is slightly varied to suit different conditions. I commence with a theme from *Joseph* (1743), which, as Professor Prout ('M. M. Record,' December, 1871) has observed, was derived from the 'Stradella' overture, 2nd movement, that is, the movement generally taking the form of a fugue, though here there is suggestion rather that achievement. The second half of the 'Stradella' quotation is a phrase which follows on the first entry of the theme; the continuation of the 'Joseph' also is given * : —

* In the case of the 'Urio' the time-values have been halved to facilitate comparison.

JOSEPH.

Joyful sounds, melo - dious strain! Health to E-gypt is the theme. Joyful sounds, melodious strain!

STRADELLA.

UTRECHT.

And we wor - - ship Thy name

URIO.

ALTO.

In te Do - mi - ne spe - ra - vi

Observe that the 'Joseph' form is just as like the 'Utrecht' (1713), as it is like the 'Stradella.' This points naturally to a possible connexion between the 'Utrecht' and 'Stradella,' and indeed in any case we should suspect it, for there is some similarity of structure in the two movements. In particular the irregularity of the first entries should be noted; the 'Stradella' falls unexpectedly to the dominant, instead of the tonic; the 'Utrecht' rises here to the third, and yet reproduces later on in the upper violin part that curious drop to the dominant. We are justified in saying that the 'Utrecht' was probably derived from the 'Stradella.'

Now up to 1713 Handel's compositions had been mainly secular. Excluding the 'Erba' and 'Urio,' the last church music he had composed, so far as is known, was the chorus for two choirs at the end of the 'N. D.,' 'et in saecula saeculorum, Amen.' * The words which follow

---

* This concluding chorus is not contained in the German Handel Society's edition, but may be found in Novello's pianoforte score.

'And we worship thy name,' in the 'Utrecht' movement, are, of course, 'ever world without end,' *i.e.*, 'in saecula saeculorum.' Can it be by accident, then, that we find our theme again in this 'N. D.' chorus, in conjunction with another? It is indeed only at bar 8 (here quoted) that we find the exact resemblance (this being also the first regular entry), as in other places the theme is only used to set the word 'Amen,' and has to lose the opening dotted crotchet in consequence. At the first entry (not quoted) the theme irregularly *rises* to the dominant, where the 'Stradella' falls. I have continued the quotation to show the resemblance to the 'Joseph' movement :—

Bar 33 shows the slight variation which brings it near the 'Urio' form :—

Remark now a further curious link between the 'N. D.' and 'Stradella.' At the end of the 'Stradella' there is a sort of *coda,* of which we quote a fragment :—

STRADELLA.

And in the ' N. D.' after a time the themes are deserted for similar ejaculations, quaver and crotchet:—

N. D.

SOPRANO. 2nd Choir.

ALTO. 1st Choir.

BASS. 2nd Choir.

Observe the upward rise in each on the resumption. The ' Urio ' chorus also has its ejaculations, though they only occur prominently in the last bar but four, when for a bar and a half they are of the same character as those quoted. On the other hand when the chorus was adapted for *Saul* as ' Retrieve the Hebrew name,' these ejaculations became a striking feature.

Looking at the phenomena together, we are justified in regarding a connexion between the ' Stradella ' and ' N. D.'—the ' Urio ' too in a less degree—as highly probable. The ' Stradella ' theme is, of course, the only fugue-like theme in the whole work, a circumstance which emphasises the coincidence and diminishes proportionally the chances of accident.

So far there is nothing to show whether the ' Stradella ' or the ' N. D.' was the first written. Let us see if we can get help from a still earlier work, the 1704 *Passion*. Of this and of its most important fugal chorus, Handel

II.

must have had a lively recollection; in fact, there is independent reason to believe that it was in his mind in Italy, and probably a month or two before he wrote the 'N. D.'* It is, therefore, as certain as need be that he was aware of the resemblance between this 'N. D.' chorus and the *Passion* chorus referred to. It is a resemblance, not only of theme but of counterpoint. The key is D minor :—

This brings us face to face with the possibility of the *Passion* and 'Stradella' being connected. It is clear that if the 'N. D.' theme was derived from the *Passion*, so might also the 'Stradella' be derived, notwithstanding the substitution of the 4th for the 6th between bars 1 and 2. And here again we are not without a further unexpected resemblance, which strengthens the suspicion. That curious drop to the dominant in the 'Stradella' form explains itself as being necessary, if the second little phrase is not to enter rather ineptly. But why was a second subject selected which created the difficulty? It is not a counterpoint to the first theme, but it appears separately twice more taking this form :—

---

* See p. 214. For the purpose of our argument, it is sufficient that Handel was acquainted with this *Passion*. The authorship is discussed in note D, p. 211.

Now in the *Passion* chorus the counterpoint quoted above is found in the exposition * only and never reappears, but its place is taken by another phrase which follows on the last entry in the exposition, and is prominent for the rest of the movement. It forms, therefore, in the structure the nearest possible analogue to the ' Stradella ' phrase :—

PASSION.

tei - - len son - dern drum lo - sen

The last note but one varies between a minim and a crotchet, and the drop at the end between a sixth and a fourth.   Observe that the phrase is introduced by an upward leap of an octave, which would have been impossible in the ' Stradella,' as it would have taken the violin part too high. This sudden introduction, then, the short uncommon form rather melodic than contrapuntal, the minim or its equivalent followed by two quavers, the drop at the end, these resemblances in analogous subsidiary phrases, resemblances which chance would not produce once in a thousand times, in view of the vast number of ways of continuing a subject, make the likelihood of ' accident ' very small.†

Next may be quoted the subject of the 5-part chorus, an irregular sort of fughetta, in the ' Urio,' the time-values having been halved as in the previous ' Urio ' chorus. The key is A, though with a G natural at first.

---

* 'That part of the Fugue during which the voices make their first entries in succession, and which extends as far as the conclusion of the subject or answer (as the case may be) by the voice that enters last.'   E. Prout. *Fugue.*

† The 'Stradella' phrase *might* (not *must*) have been derived from the ' Passion' phrase; and you might search long, high and low, in similar places, before finding anything of which so much could be said. That is the real significance.

Observe the imitation at the interval of a minim. Owing to this imitation the descent must in any case have been cut short. But when the shackle is removed, we find the second treble entering thus, Bar 6 :—

So that the *Passion* subject (previously cut short) has now reappeared with just those slight modifications, which the difference of words demanded; the counterpoint having, of course, shown itself at the first two entries as part of the subject. But this counterpoint, or part of the subject, disappears even more quickly than in the *Passion* chorus; the other voices, which enter at bar 6, when the first two have finished their imitation, leave it out entirely. A very unusual structure is thus given to the chorus, to which, as remarked above, I have found only one parallel, viz., the 5-part ' Wretched lovers,' *Acis,* the subject of which exhibits a slight resemblance in the curve and the opening cretic (long short long) rhythm, a rhythm not very common at the beginning of a fugue subject. The return journey from *Acis* will form the subject of the next section.

III.

Let me quote from the duet ' Happy we ' (*Acis*), the number which originally preceded ' Wretched lovers '— the chorus ' Happy we ' was a later addition. The quotation is from the return to the first section (after the *da capo*) including the opening voice-phrase :—

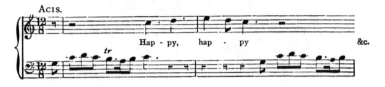

Compare now the corresponding passage—the return to the opening voice-phrase—in the ' Urio ' duet, ' Tu rex gloriae,' which *immediately succeeds* the above chorus ' Sanctum quoque '; this duet has a three-section form, returning to the first opening but without a strict *da capo* :—

As in the *Acis* the two violins and oboes play in unison over the bass, so in the ' Urio ' we find the two violins and violettas *all' ottava* on the line above the bass. A certain resemblance at the opening of the voice-parts of the second sections in the two duets is also worth noting :—

In each case the quotations exhibit the only *new* features of the second sections. Now turn to the ' Stradella ' overture *third* movement, which I had independently noted as connected with ' Happy we.' * The opening bars are quoted : —

STRADELLA.

&c.

What a strong appearance there is here of an instrumental introduction leading up to a voice-phrase in the upper part of bars 5 and 6, quite on the lines of the *Acis* and ' Urio ' with their lengthy instrumental introductions ! Indeed the whole of this instrumental portion appears to be constructed so as to harmonise with this voice-phrase ; and yet, curiously enough, this voice-phrase never appears again, nor is there anything in the remotest degree resembling it ; moreover, the phrases of bar 3, which are clearly intended to harmonise with the voice-phrase at bar 6, never once reappear. It is the 6-note germ of bar 1, and the other phrase of bar 2, which are treated at length. This structure is curious, but receives its explanation, when we examine the air which *immediately precedes* the *Passion* chorus. The voice-part of this has the time-signature C, over a 12-8 bass. The alteration has been made to facilitate comparison. The bass continuation at the end of the

* See p. 116.

quotation represents, not what stands where the voice-phrase is first given, but what appears when it is repeated after the usual Scarlattian false start :—

The curious resemblance of the prominent words 'Du . . Rock ' ' Tu rex ' will not escape notice. After the opening, the voice-phrase is (like the ' Urio ' phrase) never repeated till after the *da capo;* this is common, however, in Handel's early works. It is the 6-note germ on which the movement is really constructed. And observe that if Handel wished to reverse the 6 note *Passion* germ, so as still to harmonise with the voice-part, it would have to be modified precisely as in the last bar of our *Passion* quotation. Reverse that, and you get (in quavers throughout, of course) the ' Stradella ' germ.

These minutiae are, I am afraid, calculated to vex the soul of the hasty thinker. Movements in triple time, he might say, based on a germ of 6 notes, are not so very uncommon; is there not one in that well-known work of Bach's, the ' 48,' Prelude 9, one decidedly like the ' Stradella ' form? True, so there is, but then, (*a*) this could not have been developed from the *Passion* germ; (*b*) there is no resemblance whatever of voice-phrase; (*c*) a hunt had to be made for it.

I noted previously (p. 119) the reason for thinking that

in ' Happy we ' Handel had primarily this *Passion* air
in his mind, though the actual form is more like that of
the ' Urio,' or ' Stradella.' In some respects, however,
the general accompaniment comes nearer to the *Passion*
air, and it comes still nearer to that of the form this
Passion air took in *Il Trionfo* (probably April—June,
1707 *). It is worth while to quote from this later development, as it leaves no doubt about Handel's acquaintance
with the *Passion,* nor that it was in his mind in Italy.
The quotation is from the opening of the voice-part :—

Il Trionfo.

Ven-gail Tem-po e con l'a - li   funes - te

Here again we meet with the extremely uncommon
feature of a voice-part marked C over a 12-8 part for *bassi*
alone (no instruments) ; the same key, B flat ; the same general
structure ; a six-note accompanying germ, very similar,
and repeated first a third and then a fifth lower, and an
opening voice-phrase which—apart from the first note,
which the Italian words have to reject—commences in the
same way.

IV.

Before attempting to estimate the force of these resemblances, let us look at the duets between canto and basso,
referred to on p. 117. The extracts exhibit the three and
only phrases to which the opening words, ' Eterna fac
cum sanctis tuis,' of the ' Urio ' duet are set; and the
three prominent phrases of the first half of the ' Stradella '
duet. These may be said to represent the thematic material
of the voice-parts, and occur in the same order. As the
first two in each are continuous, they are quoted together.

* See note E, p. 212.

It will be observed that the extracts up to the end of the second phrase in each are of precisely the same length :—

The third phrases exhibit a relationship corresponding to that between the second pair :—

The canto in the ' Urio ' throughout this passage sings a third (or tenth) higher. Both movements contain the same kind of long-winded cadences. It will, I think, be agreed that the whole resemblance is decidedly stronger than that between Steffani's duet and Handel's chorus, quoted p. 131. The fact of both being duets for canto and basso; the repetition of opening words; the equality in length being continued up to the end of the second phrase; the resemblance between third phrases; these things make the unlikelihood of accident greater than in the other case, which is yet generally accepted. Let us make a calculation now on the principles explained above, pp. 128-9. Certainly not one movement in ten on an average is a duet between canto and basso; still I shall be content to take this figure. We have then $10 \times 10 \times 10 \times 10 = 10,000$; this duet resemblance might have happened accidentally once in 10,000 trials. By successive multiplications we shall get the figures for the whole of the phenomena exhibited by the *Passion,* ' Urio,' and ' Stradella '; $10,000 \times 22,500$ (*Passion* —' Stradella ') $\times 22,500$ (*Passion*—' Urio ') $\times 30$ [because the consecutive themes (*Passion*—' Stradella ') are the *same* pair as those (*Passion*—' Urio ')—there were 30 possible pairs in the *Passion*] $\times 40$ (?), (because of the resemblance of words between the ' Urio ' duet and *Passion* air; the figure is pretty certainly too low). Then $10,000 \times 22,500 \times 22,500 \times 30 \times 40 = 6075,000000,000000$. In this calculation no account has been taken of the resemblance between the ' Stradella ' fugue-theme, the ' N. D.' chorus and the final ' Urio ' chorus, and yet something has happened which would not occur by accident once in 6 thousand million million trials.* Such a romantic experience we should not be justified in imputing to Handel, even were there strong evidence in its support; and, in fact, as will

* In the article 'S.I.M.G.', viii, p. 574, the second 'million' was omitted through error

be shown later, there is no real evidence whatever. Some part of the phenomena at least cannot be accidental.

Are we to suppose then that Padre Urio borrowed from the ' Stradella,' and presented both works to Handel in Italy ? Such presentations are rare, and would not account for the resemblances to the *Passion*. Or did he despatch both works to Handel at Hamburg, where Handel extracted those duller *Passion* forms from them ? Or did he send only the *Te Deum* (a class of work, by the bye, which rarely circulated) and did chance fling the ' Stradella ' afterwards in Handel's path ? In any case this would not account for the features absent from the ' Urio,' in which the *Passion* is akin to the ' Stradella.' Every explanation, in short, involves wild improbabilities, except that to which no objection whatever can be taken—Handel's authorship of the ' Urio ' *Te Deum.**

The chances of ' accident ' in the case of the ' Stradella ' alone—once in 22,500 trials—are not so forlorn. I do not think anyone is likely to suggest seriously that the *Passion* forms were developed from the ' *Stradella* '; the ' accident ' theory would be accorded the preference. Still such accidents are rare, and the evidence should be remarkably strong to make us comfortable in such a conclusion. On the other hand we can trace the gradual development of the ' Stradella ' fugue-theme through the ' N. D.,' and the gradual enlivening of the *Passion* 12-8 movement in ' Venga il tempo' (*Il Trionfo*), and perhaps in ' Là ti sfido ' (*Rodrigo*), the special features of construction also in the ' Stradella ' thus finding their explanation.

---

* In the consideration of possible solutions *all* the phenomena must be steadily kept in mind. Besides the key-move in a chess-problem there are many brilliant solutions, or rather there would be, if we could only forget that miserable knight or bishop.

CHAPTER XVII.

' URIO ' TE DEUM.

THERE are three known ' Urio ' MSS., all of which may
be regarded as of English origin. For this is certain of
two of them, hereafter called A and C; and though Sir
George Grove [Dictionary, s.v. Urio] said the third, B,
was certainly in an Italian hand, Mr. Barclay Squire kindly
gives his opinion that all appearances suggest rather an
English hand or hands; part indeed may be in that of the
possessor, Stafford Smith. Now C claims that it was
copied from an Italian manuscript that had once been in
Handel's possession, but was owned at the time of copying
by Dr. Samuel Howard (who died 1782). We may, with
sufficient confidence for our purpose, regard this last MS.
as the archetype of all three, without deciding whether it
was written by an Italian, or by Handel, who himself wrote
an Italian hand while in Italy. Any theory, which required
more than one English archetype, would saddle itself with a
large improbability to start with, to gain no advantage
worth mentioning. A description of the relevant headings
or notes will be given; but I shall omit a number of entries,
which can throw no possible light on the origin, and merely
testify to the interest felt by the possessors.

A. Now in the Conservatoire National (Paris); the
name of E. T. Warren is appended at the end, so that
presumably he was the copyist. Whether he was identical
with the E. T. Warren Horne, who possessed the MS., I
have not been able to ascertain. After Warren Horne's
death it was in the possession of J. W. Callcott in 1797.
E. T. Warren died, I understand, in 1794.

There is only one heading, over the top of the score on
the first page. This runs:—

      Te Deum   Urio 1660

Everyone will reject this 1660, I think. Dates seem to be affixed on MSS. with a nonchalance equal to that of Cap'en Cuttle, when naming the authors of his quotations.* It is impossible for Handel, certainly; and F. A. Urio cannot really be supposed to have written a remarkable work 30 years before publishing his Op. 1 in 1690. Moreover, such a work by anyone at that date would have been a veritable marvel. Another practically fatal objection is that the date does not appear on the other MSS., though one of them makes a gallant attempt on its own account, ' apud 1682.' We have a right, therefore, to reject the date, and dismiss it from our calculations. And observe that if the date had been more than a guess the person who knew it might have been expected also to know something about ' Padre F. A.' (Urio). But in fact it is shown clearly by the blank space above that there was no such prefix on the archetype, else the space would not have been left blank. It must have been ' Urio ' without further addition.

B.   Now in the R. C. M., London, and formerly in the possession of Stafford Smith in 1780, as the cover states. This information on the cover, certainly written by Smith, proceeds—' by Urio—a Jesuit of Bologna, apud 1682.' Observe first that apud (=about) could not have been written by Padre Urio or anyone having first-hand information; the date must be, like the 1660, purely decorative. It will not be contended that ' a Jesuit of Bologna ' was written on an Italian MS.† The really significant circumstance here is that ' Urio ' has no initials. And now let us turn to the heading placed, like the heading of A, over the top of the score. This reads ' Te Deum Con due Trombe,

* Of a *Miserere* of Scarlatti's the Abbé Santini in 1824 made two copies; one is dated 1705, the other 1714. Mr. Dent, *Alessandro Scarlatti*, p. 113, thinks neither date at all probable.

† The use of 'Jesuit' is very likely connected with the Lord George Gordon riots in 1780; there was just then a great outcry against Jesuits. Every priest would be termed Jesuit.

due Oboe, Violini & due Viole obligati & Fagotto à 5 vo[ci] Urio.' So that we have the same heading as A, minus the date, except that the blank space is filled up by a description of the instruments. which may or may not be original.

So far, then, we have found no reason to suppose that E. T. Warren or Stafford Smith had discovered anything about ' Padre F. A.' on the archetype. But it may be, of course, that the more youthful eyes of John Anderson, a chorister of St. Paul's, who made our next copy in 1781, were keener.

C. This 1781 copy by Anderson, now in the British Museum, has no heading over the top of the score. But on the outer cover it reads :—' Te Deum Laudamus con due Trombe, due Oboe et Violini et due Viole obligati, Del Padre Fra͠nco Uria [*sic*] Bolognese.' Here information simply rushes in a torrent; and yet I do not feel convinced. For if this interesting information *did* stand on the archetype how came the sand-blind Warren and Smith to overlook it? Of course it might be explained that it was not there originally, but that it was a later and perfectly genuine discovery. Still, to be genuine, this must mean that some one put the MS. in his pocket and scoured Italy to find another copy, and make comparisons; a possible but arduous enterprise. I will venture to suggest that a much easier course was taken. A man there was at Bologna, whose authority on antiquarian matters was preeminent, Padre Martini, in touch with English musicians, and a correspondent of Burney's. It was perfectly simple to write to him for information about some mysterious ' Urio.' And the result was scarcely doubtful. Martini's library passed after his death to the Liceo Musicale, Bologna. In that library are now to be found copies of Padre Urio's Op. 1 and Op. 2, the latter having been printed at Bologna. So now our 'Bolognese' and 'of Bologna ' are explained, and explanation they certainly needed. For Padre Urio was *not* ' Bolognese '; he says himself distinctly in the title of his Op. 1 that he was ' da Milano.'

Fortunately this inquiry, which we have inferred from the MSS. phenomena, receives external support, though this was, strictly, unnecessary. The kindness of Monsieur Julien Tiersot has informed me that at the foot of the first page of the Paris MS. is found a note written to all appearance by the hand of the original copyist, E. T. Warren:—' Francesco Antonio Urio was Maestro di Capella at Venice. He published at Bologna in the year 1697 Salmi concertati.' This proves that people in England *did* take the course indicated; they made inquiries and heard of these ' Salmi concertati,' Op. 2, published at Bologna. E. T. Warren, as before observed, died in 1794, and there is no reason to suppose that this note was not already written by 1781.

By every canon of criticism then we are warranted in assuming that the only thing relevant on the archetype, and the only thing we have a right to consider, is the words ' Te Deum   Urio.' The space between may or may not have been filled by a description of the instruments.* Of course, escape from this conclusion is perfectly easy if we assume sufficient abnormality and eccentricity in our copyists. But to scurry to such a refuge would be to abandon the whole case. This case for Padre Urio depends on manuscript testimony alone; and that would not be worth a straw, if copyists may be supposed abnormal when it becomes convenient. It would be just as easy to say that someone put on ' Urio ' ' for fun,' and dismiss the whole subject.

An appeal to manuscripts implies or should imply a

---

* Probably not; observe the differences in the two lists. C gives just those instruments used on the first page. B may have noticed that the Fagotto was used later. If there was a date originally, it must have been no longer legible.

willingness to abide by ' the rules of the game.' To those
rules Dr. Chrysander and Mr. Sedley Taylor appealed,
and I think very rightly, in order to reject the ' possessor '
interpretation of ' Del R^d Sig^r Erba.' It would contradict
universal or almost universal manuscript practice. But
when it is proposed to make ' Urio ' mean a composer, we
too are entitled to ask for precedents for such a thing on
a formal Italian MS.; for if not formal, of what value can
it be as evidence? We have no Christian name, no
initials, no ' Padre,' we have not even a preposition ' di.'
No one can prove an universal negative, and I shall not
assert that no precedent can be found; but even great un-
commonness should prevent our interpreting it in this way,
unless all other interpretations are still worse supported;
and even then as evidence it would be almost valueless.
What can the testimony of a ' freak ' be worth? And
observe that if we supposed Handel to have got his copy
from Padre Urio direct, the difficulty would only be
increased. How could Padre Urio, or a copyist writing
under his direction, have used such a form?

Even if Handel's authorship had not been demonstrated
in the previous chapter, an alternative explanation to a
practical nullity would really be unnecessary. Still an
explanation will be offered, which seems perfectly unobjectionable, and more than this no one can expect. When
we find 'Cannons 171-,' 'Gotha, 1812,' 'Düsseldorf,
1707,'* on MSS. written by Haym, Weber, and Steffani
respectively—of course the examples might be increased
indefinitely—we feel no temptation to conjure up visions
of Cannons, Gotha, or Düsseldorf essaying the rôle of
composer. And yet, had Haym's MS. found its way to
Italy, this might have happened, for an Italian copyist
would be very unlikely to have ever heard of Cannons.
Now in 1700 there was a place, Urio, of considerable

---

* This last MS., the opera *Arminio*, bears no composer's name. About
the others I am unable to say.

antiquity, I am informed. The name is believed to have
been derived from the Latin ' urere,' on account of a big
fire that once occurred there. It lies on the lake, about 6
miles north of Como, and faces the celebrated Villa
Pliniana. No more objection can be raised to Handel's
staying there, than to his staying at Barn Elms in 1713,
or at Gopsal with Jennens, or to Wagner's staying at
Triebschen. A letter of Handel's addressed from Urio, a
mention of such a stay by Mainwaring—with these at our
disposal, no one would feel at all puzzled, or propose to
regard the letter as a forgery. It must be, therefore, quite
unobjectionable as an explanation of the meaning of the
MS. If it were urged as an objection, that no date is
added to ' Urio,' so as to make a complete parallel to the
examples quoted, it might be answered first, that nobody
would reject the interpretation in the other cases, even
were there no date; and secondly that there may have been
originally a date on the archetype.   In the example
' Cannons, 171-,'' the last figure is illegible; it is quite
possible that here also were some illegible figures. Without
laying stress on the point, let us remark that 1709 might
easily be misread as 1760, and this being perceived to be
impossible would result in the ' correction ' 1660; or it
might have been originally written through carelessness
1609; or an ill-formed 7 might be mistaken for a 6—there
is a doubt as to one of Handel's early Italian MSS.,
whether the reading should be 4 or 11. Or 1660 may have
been derived from something like 'Roma Il dì 3 di Marzzo'
which we find on an Italian cantata.   On one MS.
possessed by Bach, the only thing now decipherable in
what was presumably the heading is ' d L.' However,
with or without date, Roma, Milano, Urio, Cannons,
imply naturally a place, not a composer.

That Handel should be staying in the neighbourhood
of Lake Como and be writing a *Te Deum* about May, 1709,
we have a right otherwise to regard as a plausible

suggestion. European peace was just then most confidently anticipated; indeed the proposed articles were already published by the expectant victors.* Handel might well have been commissioned by the Austrians to write a *Te Deum* for Milan, their headquarters in Italy. In advance such a *Te Deum* might easily be written, just as he prepared the ' Utrecht ' *Te Deum* before the conclusion of peace, precisely as in quite recent years Sir Arthur Sullivan prepared a *Te Deum* long before it was required. And that Handel *did* write music for this expected but never realised peace, is sufficiently proved by the cantata, *Io languisco,* which introduces the high gods and goddesses bringing peace to mortals, and rest to the warriors. Those who care to examine the point will acquiesce, I have little doubt, in this date and occasion for the cantata, and agree that Milan was far the most likely place for the proposed performance.† A possible independent point of connexion between this cantata and the *Te Deum* was noted, p. 119; and it may be added that the aria ' Se qui il Ciel,' or its equivalent in *Apollo e Dafne,* is the one movement among Handel's cantatas which I had previously remarked as having a resemblance to anything in the ' Urio,' the ' Salvum fac populum.' ‡ That besides the cantata Handel should write a *Te Deum,* the main feature in peace celebrations, might in any case have been expected; in fact did not the ' Urio ' survive, it would be almost necessary to invent it.

If it should be asked why Handel should have stayed at Urio of all places near Milan, the reason might be the same which induced him to stay at Barn Elms, the

---

* Abbé, *Dictionnaire des Cardinaux*, s. v. Albani.

† See note C, p. 204.

‡ The ' Te per orbem, however, may have been suggested by the air in *Agrippina* and *La Resurrezione,* ' Ho un non so che,' the melody of which (see note p. 71) Herr Schering has traced to Corelli. The violins in the ' Urio' appear to take over the vocal melody, while the voice seems to utilise Handel's instrumental interludes.

residence of a Mr. Andrews, in 1713, viz., that he was
invited to stay there. Urio lies in a pleasant situation on
Lake Como. The modern ' Castello di Urio,' now in the
possession of Mrs. MacCreery, was acquired in 1834 by
Count Melzi (from the family Castelbarco), as I am
informed by Signor Carlo Ciceri, the librarian of Her
Excellency the Duchess Melzi, to whose kindness I am
much indebted. I have no reason to suppose that the villa
was not in existence in 1709, though the courteous present
owner has not yet been able to find precise information.
In 1709 the ' luogotenente cesareo,' the imperial representative, was Count Sforza Lodovico Melzi. The music was
perhaps written at his request, but as the Castelbarco family
were also then prominent in the Austrian *régime* at Milan,
Handel might very well stay at their villa when writing
the *Te Deum*.* The explanation then is quite unobjectionable, and as it fully satisfies the MS. data, nothing
more can be desired. To demand independent proof of
a stay at Urio would be to forget that there is no evidence
whatever that Padre Urio ever wrote any, much less this,
Te Deum, or that if he did, Handel was ever within
twenty leagues of a copy.

There is no plausibility in the theory of Padre Urio
having written a work of an elaboration quite unusual in
those days. No extant work of Alessandro Scarlatti
exhibits such elaboration. If Urio had received a commission to write such a work, it could only be because
his reputation stood very high. Yet of this there is no
trace. He enjoyed the patronage extended to most composers of that day, the patronage of Cardinal Ottoboni,
and of Ferdinand dei Medici; for Ferdinand he wrote some
works, the last recorded being the oratorio, *Maddalena
convertita* (1706); but there is no indication of his ever
emerging from the rank and file. Whether in matters of
form and small details the work corresponds with what

* Of course, Handel's stay may have been at some other house.

might have been expected from Pedre Urio, no one can say; it agrees, however, with what might have been expected from Handel. Having only late English copies, we are not entitled, I think, to lay stress on minutiæ.

Whether anyone will feel a difficulty as to style, the work having been written after Handel had been more than two years in Italy, and for popular rejoicings, I cannot say. A marked inclination towards Italian style and feelings was to be expected; yet Professor Prout's observation about the strong Handelian character of one air * seems applicable to the whole work, and a note on the Paris MS., made probably by Monsieur Schoelcher, says that the work was admired in England, the style of the counterpoint being ' particularly English.' Sir George Grove (Dict., s.v. Urio) thought the merits of the *Te Deum* were considerable and Dr. Gauntlett, I infer, regarded the counterpoint as too good to be Handel's. But Mr. W. S. Rockstro, having a theory that the work was a late compilation, introducing fragments from *Saul* and the *Dettingen Te Deum,* laid stress on the want of continuity exhibited in the work. I think most people will agree, first, that he much exaggerated this alleged want of continuity, and secondily, that, as remarked by Dr. Chrysander in connexion with *Agrippina,* Handel acquired a much surer touch in this respect after his Italian period. The fact is, that when we have been accustomed to strains in one context, their appearance in another always seems at first unnatural. In the particular illustration given by Mr. Rockstro, the opening movement, the first strain of the instrumental introduction is really a representation of carillons; naturally the connexion with the other portions cannot be expected to be as close as usual. It is comparable rather to the interludes in a Bach chorale. And to take the work as a whole, the doubt might rather arise, whether

* See above, p. 124.

any composer of that era, Handel excepted, could command the continuity exhibited.

In the absence of specific objections to style in the case of the ' Urio ' (if there are thought to be any), as equally in the case of the ' Erba,' detailed discussion becomes impossible. So far indeed as historical or quasi-ethical objections are concerned, the answer is not difficult. Chrysander objected to the ' Italianisation ' of the ' Erba '; this Italianisation was absent from the Roman psalms (probably written in part in Germany), April—July, 1707, and appeared first in the ' Utrecht ' music (1713). But then there is no extant church music of Handel's between these two dates, except the ' Erba ' and ' Urio,' so where else could Italianisation be found? Unless this feature came like ' a bolt from the blue ' into the ' Utrecht ' music, where, however, Handel was deliberately imitating Purcell, the existence of some works such as these two, written before he left Italy, seems almost presupposed. Chrysander's second objection is very curious; Handel, it appears, would have had some mysterious scruples about adopting the style of Italian church music, while in Italy. Most certainly such scruples had been thoroughly exorcised when he wrote *Israel* (1738). Perhaps, when formulating the objection (i, 166) Chrysander was as yet unacquainted with the *Salve Regina,* and the cantata *con stromenti, Ah che troppo;* at any rate, he neglected to reconcile this opinion with the remark at i, 219, that the chorus 'Son larve di dolor ' in *Il Trionfo* (1707-8) was modelled on Italian church music [' bei dem die italienischen Kirchen-stücke Vorbild waren '].

By the bye, the only chorus to those words, that I can find, is that which is now credited to Graun. Did Chrysander fail to distinguish between Handel and Graun? He perceived, however, as must in fairness be added, a difference in style between this chorus and Handel's later works. The chorus is fine, said he, but ' nicht so völlig

in sich gerundet ' as these. He did not question Handel's
authorship, nor can he be blamed, I think, for this.
Differences in style are readily observed; it is quite easy
to espy differences between *The Tempest, The Merchant
of Venice,* and *The Comedy of Errors.* But to decide
that an author could not possibly have written in a certain
style, to measure nicely the exact length of the chain which
circumscribes his wanderings, is not every man's business.
It requires courage, inflamed by youth and undamped by
experience, to lay down that Shakespeare *could* not have
written *Titus Andronicus,* if he had had the mind. I am
not sure that confident pronouncements about style are
not ' against the public interest.' For if we are thoroughly
in earnest, who will be safe? That man's symphony may
be taken away, for it is too good to be his; another man's
opera, for he could never have written anything so bad;
Tennyson's *Northern Farmer* must be a plagiarism, for
it is not in the style of his *Princess;* and Shelley's ' Widow
Bird ' must be restored to Wordsworth. It is a common
complaint that when a man has written well in one style,
it is difficult for him to gain acceptance for works written
in a different manner; but how miserable his position, if
his authorship of the later works may be jauntily denied!
Perhaps Bononcini did not exactly remember writing the
madrigal, but judged ' from the style ' that it must be
his own, and could not possibly be Lotti's.

However, experience cannot conceal the fact that the
best authorities are generally in frank opposition. Mendelssohn and Schumann flatly disagreed about Bach's (?)
St. Luke Passion. Is *The Phoenix and the Turtle* by
Shakespeare? Had he a hand in *The Two Noble Kins-
men?* Of this play Shelley did not believe he wrote one
word. Coleridge was confident on the opposite side;
Tennyson thought it contained a good deal of Shakespeare. Are some dances, recently discovered, really by
Beethoven? Is a recently unearthed violin concerto really

by Mozart? These are not supposed to be early works, yet opinions array themselves one against the other.

After all, Handel thought it worth while to bring away and carefully preserve these compositions. If they were, in his opinion, inferior works by obscure composers, what was his motive for making this curious selection? And if they were fine works, in his opinion, written in an unobjectionable style, no difficulty remains in the supposition that he cultivated the style himself while in Italy.

CHAPTER XVIII.

' STRADELLA ' SERENATA.

I.

(1) THE undated MS. presented by Monsieur Schoelcher to the Conservatoire National, Paris,* where it is now lodged, was assigned by Chrysander an origin in Italy in the closing decades of the seventeenth century. The only reasons given are the ' clear and almost faultless copy.' [Preface to his edition.] The grounds of this confidence I do not understand. Let some decree, dated 1700, be produced, which enforces with severe penalties deterioration in accuracy and style of handwriting, and then light might begin to dawn. But if experience be any guide, a boy who in 1710 was 15 years old and wrote in the style customary about 1700, might still be writing in precisely the same style in Italy or England in 1780. Copyists do not die off like summer flies. And let it be remembered that Constantine Simonides in the nineteenth century could write exactly like the ancient Greek calligraphers.

(2) The writing is considered to be Italian rather than English. This does not give us much help. In England ' the Italian hand ' was a lauded accomplishment. Moreover, there were always hosts of Italian musicians in London, including Signor Piozzi, who married Mrs. Thrale in 1784.

(3) General condition is a very uncertain indication of age; it varies with the fortunes of the manuscript; just as, before dating a brick from its colour, we must know whether it came from the pure heights of Dartmoor or from the smoke of Sheffield. Of one autograph of Scarlatti, an

* It can be traced back to the Rev. John Parker, who sold it in 1813. (*Notes and Queries*, March 6th, 1858.)

extremely fine specimen of calligraphy, Mr. Dent remarks that the pages are literally dropping to pieces.* Yet some MSS. dating from remote ages are in fair condition. Again, inferences drawn from custom must not be pressed too far. One of the chief reasons for assigning the Vatican MS. of the New Testament to the fourth century is found in the non-insertion of the Eusebian canons. Yet its own arrangement has only one parallel, and that is found in a manuscript assigned to the eighth century.

(4) Whether a cautious expert would discover sufficient grounds for a confident opinion as to date, I do not know; wide experience in these matters makes, I believe, for caution. Monsieur Julien Tiersot has kindly informed me that the ascription is written on the first page, between the staves of music, as follows :—

> Serenata a . 3 . con stromenti
>
> Del Sig^r. Alessandro Stradella

The full stop at the end is placed above the line, perhaps because there is a long, flourishing tail to the a. What may be the significance of the dots under the words, I do not know. I had previously suggested that SIGR., as Chrysander reproduced it, was more likely to be English than Italian; but both the r. and the full stop are, I find, above the line. I reproduce the heading fully; possibly someone may be able to draw an inference.

(5) It was, of course, quite possible for a work by Handel, left behind in Italy, to be ascribed by mistake to Stradella, and to find its way later to England. It is not unimportant to note that Stradella's MSS. were sold after his death, and placed in the Modena library.† With the rarest exceptions all Stradella's more important extant works are found there, and there alone. In Italy itself,

---

* *Alessandro Scarlatti*, p. 93.

† Heinz Hess, *Die Opern Alessandro Stradellas*, pp. 2, 12.

outside the Modena library, there are only some separate solo cantatas, with the addition of one copy of the oratorio *San Giovanni*. But England possesses the only two serenatas not to be found in the library at Modena, though one of them appeared in the Modena catalogue 1761. There was, in fact, a demand for Stradella's works in England, so that a serenata attributed to him was as likely as not to find its way there. Of course there is no more unlikelihood of a work by Handel being attributed to Stradella, than of Stradella's *Floridoro* being attributed under the name of *Rodrigo* to Scarlatti, or of an oratorio of Cesti's being attributed to Carissimi. If it had some outward forms, resembling features in Stradella's known works, the copyist would not be scrupulous. ' Santini, like other librarians of his time, has a tendency to ascribe to Scarlatti any anonymous composition of his period . . '*
This tendency is ubiquitous.

(6) The work, perhaps, as Chrysander suggests, is incomplete.† Yet the manuscript itself must have reproduced all that lay before it, for it ends in the middle of a page, with the word *Fine* subjoined. If incomplete it must have been made from an incomplete or imperfect original, or a copy which had lost the final bars. Now if the original were imperfect the signature would probably be missing in any case. A copy might never have recorded the name at all, or it might have been on an outer cover, which vanished with the last leaf. We should then have all the conditions most favourable to conjectural ascriptions. The subject of the work, the courting of a lady by two rivals, might recall Stradella's romantic history, and cause his name to be affixed.

II.

This serenata is apparently a thing apart. Nothing like it is found in the other works of Handel or Stradella,

---

* E. J. Dent. *Alessandro Scarlatti.* Preface viii.
† It ends abruptly; possibly, however, that was intentional.

perhaps nothing like it in the works of any known composer. Besides the main division of the instruments into the usual concertino and concerto grosso, we find the further division into *primo cocchio* and *secondo cocchio,* while the lady has a concertino of her own, *concertino della dama.* Most of us will hesitate to believe that Handel, Stradella, or any copyist wrote a word wrongly thirteen times in succession, in different places; we shall therefore discard Chrysander's 'correction' to *crocchio,* of which he could only say that the term *might* have been (not, ever was) used in music. We find in all Italian dictionaries '*cocchiata*=a serenade in coaches' . (*cocchio*≐coach). Petrocchi defines it : 'Passeggiata di sonatori notturna, e la Poesia che cantavano.' In Dr. Doran's '*Mann*' *and Manners at the court of Florence* we find *cocchiatas* mentioned several times by Walpole and Mann. ' 'Tis made by 12 cavalieri . . .' (i, p. 23). ' The lights up and down the garden had the prettiest effect immaginable. Those in the middle, for the Musick, were quite hid by the crowds that pressed about the table. . . . I can neither tell you the number nor the names of the *Dame* . . . . . ' (i, p. 93). I have not read or heard of anything else that throws light on the subject, but the following explanation may be hazarded.

We know that it was an ancient custom in Italy for parties to stroll through the streets in the evening, singing songs, and playing on instruments, such as the lute, between the verses. This practice would in time develope; larger and heavier instruments, such as the violoncello, would be thought desirable, and this would necessitate the advent of coaches, to carry the instruments and their players. The whole performance would then be called a *cocchiata,* and the instruments would be divided into first and second 'coaches.' This might often take the form of a real or pretended serenading of a lady or *dama,* the cavaliers driving up each on his coach. But again elaboration would go further. Instead of a wandering through the streets or the countryside, evening garden-parties, where a large audience might assemble, would be organised, in which a musical performance, perhaps combined with masquerading, would be the chief feature. The old terms *cocchiata, Dame,* etc., would be retained. Such seems to be the form of the entertainment described by Mann in 1741. Whether our serenata was written for such an evening performance, or for some rather simpler and earlier form, cannot, of course, be decided, but we may be sure that it was, at least nominally, a simple, inartificial, open-air entertainment, in which the instruments answered each other and the voice antiphonally.

(2) In such a form of entertainment complexity would be out of place. From this point of view the work may be called, in part, crude, as Sir Hubert Parry has styled it, *Oxf. Hist.,* iii, 181. The instrumental work is mostly plain, and no attempt is made to write a proper fugue in the second movement of the overture. Yet Stradella as well as Handel constructed fugues skilfully, and could write much more elaborately for the orchestra, when he chose; but here it would have been out of place. It may have been, in part, owing to the wish to follow older models, that the orchestral parts are written under the voice; but in any case it was necessary, five times out of seven, in order to keep the *concertino* together. Handel elsewhere occasionally writes some of the instruments under the voice, *e.g.,* ' V' adoro' (*Giulio Cesare*).

According to a common Italian custom, which long prevailed with Scarlatti, for example, and Leo (1694—1744) a flat or a sharp less than in the modern usage often marks the signature. The custom is illustrated in the extract from the *Passion,* in D minor p. 137. In *Agrippina* Handel uses only two flats for E flat major; in *Il Trionfo* two sharps for A major. In *Saul* after writing part of a chorus in G with one sharp, he changes to the open key, though the music still continues in G. The reason, no doubt, was that the 'Sanctum quoque'—see p. 139—which he is adapting, also had a sharp too few. This illustrates Handel's habit of conforming to his models; the convenience of the singers, perhaps amateurs, in the serenata, would also not be neglected by him. It is possible that some on making acquaintance with the work would query the use of 'allegra' on one occasion instead of the usual 'allegro.' But Handel sometimes used these forms in *a, e.g.,* 'pomposa,' and once elsewhere [see the cantatas with instruments, vol. ii, Chrysander's preface], he has used 'allegra.' In fine, in these matters of outward form there is nothing that justifies a hesitation in accepting Handel's authorship.

(3) But to the acceptance of Stradella's authorship there are certain obstacles. Sir Hubert Parry (*Oxf. Hist.,* iii, 182) finds 'decidedly noteworthy' the 'complete and undisguised da capo' of two songs, one, 'Seguir non voglio più,' marked *dal segno,* and another, 'Amor sempr' è avvezzo,' to which Chrysander has supplied the *da capo* which is obviously intended. But this is not all. The successive movements sung by the same voice, 'Io pur seguirò,' marked Aria *allegra,* and 'Ragion sempre addita,' marked Aria *Presto,* are really the two sections of the same air, as the examination of the verbal structure and of the rhymes shows. And in fact the latter part of 'Ragion sempre addita' is found to be 'Io pur seguirò,' repeated verbatim (music and words), except for minute alterations in the first and last bars. The reason why the repetition is written out in full, is doubtless the importance of the ritornello between the two sections. Again in another air, 'Mio petto inerme,' we find the same structure of text as in 'Amor sempr' è avvezzo.' Moreover, the second sections in the two airs are written on practically the same lines, including a finish with an expectant cadence, such as suggests the *da capo* repetition. It is scarcely credible that

a section commencing in F should finish thus in D minor
in order to plunge at once into a symphony in C major.
It is hardly disputable, therefore, that we have a case in
which the direction *da capo* has been omitted in the
original, or overlooked by the copyist. There are other
cases in which Handel has omitted the *Da Capo;* and the
Fines he regularly indicated merely by the 'pauses,' or
wrote nothing whatever, as here in the air 'Seguir non
voglio più.' In an air in *Il Trionfo,* 1707 (?) 'Un
pensiero nemico di pace,' where the violins are silent in the
second section (which has an entirely distinct idea), there
is neither *Da Capo, Fine,* nor pause. Chrysander has
supplied them in his edition.

Of the two remaining airs one, 'Basilisco allor,' does not
admit of a second section without manifest absurdity, and
in the case of the other, the first in the work, it was perhaps
considered that the lady, after the vigorous serenading,
required no second exhortation to wake up. Now it is
almost impossible to believe that a work containing this
amount, maturity, and elaboration of *da capo* practice, was
really written by Stradella. It may be doubted whether
any work written before February, 1682, the month of
Stradella's death, exhibits this maturity; and in Stradella's
known works, with perhaps one exception, there is, I
believe, no appearance of a *marked* da capo of any kind;
at least Herr Heinz Hess, who has kindly confirmed to me
the inference which is naturally drawn from his book, *Die
Opern Alessandro Stradellas,* has noticed none. There
seems to be only one instance even of aria form,* the repetition (verbatim) being written out in full; and this example,
in the oratorio *San Giovanni,* was perhaps suggested by
the words. In the oratorio *Susanna* (1681) and the serenata

---

* There is an inconvenient practice of applying the term *da capo* to this
aria form; inconvenient, that is, for the present discussion. Here we
confine ourselves to *da capos* marked as such.

Barcheggio, which claims to be Stradella's last composition, there is no single example of aria form.

The possible exception is the solo cantata (without instruments) *Seneca e Nerone,* in which occur two examples. But in any case such a work could not be a parallel to examples with changes of instruments; and neither air is marked *dal segno,* a usage which would emerge rather later than the mere *da capo.* Besides, when we consider the large number of false ascriptions—out of 700 cantatas attributed to Alessandro Scarlatti, 43 are asterisked by Mr. Dent as doubtful—the authenticity of a work should be clearly established before an inference is drawn. This work is, as I am informed by the courteous librarian, not autograph; it lies, not in the Modena library, but in the library of the Liceo Musicale, Bologna, which dates from 1798; and it is the *third* cantata attributed to Stradella, on the dismal theme of Seneca's entering the bath. It is very unusual for a composer to set three cantata texts on the same theme; on the other hand, if Stradella were known to have set the subject, an anonymous composition on the same theme might easily be regarded as his, and acquire his name. However this may be, our serenata would be quite unique in its modernity among Stradella's works, and a *cocchiata,* a simple inartificial entertainment, would seem of all fields, the least likely for new experiments.

There is a further feature worth pointing out; there is no example of the free ground-basses, which were common in Italy from *circa* 1675 to *circa* 1685, before the *Da Capo* form expelled them. Now, as Burney points out, more than half the airs in *San Giovanni,* which must be a late work, utilise this form, and Herr Hess says (p. 34) that Stradella was fond of it. Mr. Dent, on the contrary, speaks of Stradella as using the form rarely, but this difference would be easily explained, if Mr. Dent had happened to examine more of the earlier works than of the late works, which are no doubt mostly lodged at Modena.

We should rather have expected an example or two of this form in our serenata, for if supposed to date from *before* the ground-bass period, the *da capo* difficulty would certainly be fatal.

Again the overture or sinfonia is in three movements, commencing with an allegro. The composer, whether Handel or Stradella, would no doubt write as was customary in such works, and if Stradella never used this form elsewhere, as would seem to be the case, we must not press the point too far; indeed, the same might be said, I think, of Handel. It is a little singular, all the same, that the form is that of the Italian sinfonia or overture, which was much in use about 1700, and survived till late in the eighteenth century; it was favoured by Scarlatti, but apparently little or not at all in use in Stradella's time. Though we may not be justified in asserting on these grounds dogmatically, that Stradella could not possibly have written such a work, yet all appearances, it may be said with fairness, point to a date twenty or more years later than his death.

(4) External and circumstantial evidence, then, cast their votes overwhelmingly in favour of Handel. Let us face fairly what Stradella's authorship would require: (*a*) That this serenata, though a late work, somehow escaped transference with all the other important works—except one, a serenata at Cambridge for two voices only, which may be an early work—to the library at Modena. (*b*) That despite the simple character of a *cocchiata* it was chosen out for the display of an extent and maturity of *da capoism,* certainly quite unapproached by any other of Stradella's works, perhaps unparalleled by any work at all as early as February, 1682. (*c*) By some good hap this work fell in Handel's way, quite early in his Italian stay, and was bought by, or presented to him. (*d*) That the very unusual, perhaps unprecedented experience occurred to him, of finding in it two consecutive movements with a resemblance

to two consecutive movements in one of his two extant, previously written, works of importance. [These are all that can be considered; it is possible that the lost works, *Nerone,* and *Florindo e Dafne*, supplied a quantity of material for the Serenata.] These resemblances it is certain that he recognised, if we assume his authorship of the ' Urio '; and indeed it would be otherwise probable through the use of the ' Urio ' or ' Stradella ' in *Acis* immediately after the 1716 *Passion* (see p. 119).

On the other hand, the acquisition of a wrong name by a manuscript is a very common occurrence. Of two evils, we are told, the less should be chosen; and of two improbabilities surely the less, in our case immeasurably the less, should be favoured. Handel's authorship is by far the more probable theory.

(5) But how about style, it may be asked; is the style such as we should expect from Handel, writing an imitative *cocchiata,* perhaps introducing an archaism or two? It is notorious that he imitated Purcell and Steffani; it is notorious that when in Italy he wrote carefully-modelled French songs, and probably also a Spanish song; it is also notorious that is is often difficult to distinguish between imitations and the thing imitated : ' there are passages in some of his [Scarlatti's] work of this kind which might easily be mistaken, even by experts, for inspirations of Palestrina himself ' (*Oxf. Hist.*, iii, 400).

On this subject of style I may be permitted to refer again to some remarks on pp. 156-8. Personally I can discern no difficulty. The long-winded cadences in the duet 'Amiche, nemiche,' for instance, are paralleled, if parallel be needed, in the corresponding ' Urio ' duet. One little progression, bars 35, etc., is, no doubt, an archaism : but if such things were fatal, 'Hear, Jacob's God' (*Samson*) would have to be rejected. The fact is, there are certainly intentional crudities in the work. Observe the *sinfonia* in the middle of the work; the orchestra of the lady has cadences with consecutive seconds, but the opposing orchestra never uses them. They appear also in the neighbouring airs of the lady, and are intended, beyond doubt, to represent her severity.* This cadence is used frequently in the 1704 *Passion* to express grief; and it appears occasionally in later works, in *Silla*, in *Giulio Cesare*, and at the close of the sinfonia in *Admeto*, where Hercules clubs the furies. There is a still more formidable dissonance of this character at the end of *Rodrigo*. It was, in fact, reserved by Handel for special effects, just as he not infrequently, in early works more particularly, used consecutive fifths for special expression of words. In the Recitative, p. 18, of the serenata consecutive octaves are employed to mark 'veleno' = poison (cf. p. 27); to this again there are several parallels in Handel, *e.g.*, the consecutive unisons in a Recitative of the cantata *Nell' Africane selve*, p. 172, bars 8–10. In *Aci*, in the air 'Sibilar l' angui,' consecutive unisons happen to be used to express the same word 'velen(o).'

Of course, with the general style of Italian works about 1680 Handel would probably have some acquaintance before he came to Italy. Carlo Pallavicino, for instance, was engaged at Dresden, dying there 1688. And Handel would have had no scruples in conforming to the requirements of the entertainment. When it was proper for him to write simple voice-phrases, to be echoed by the instruments, he would do it, without dragging in contrapuntal elaboration.

* An apparent instance in 'Io pur seguirò' is shown by the corresponding passage to be due to a slip of the pen.

CHAPTER XIX.

'Erba' Magnificat.

I.

Of the 'Erba' *Magnificat* two MSS. are in existence. One, which was never completed, is in Handel's writing, and bears no composer's name; it has been assigned, on what seem sufficient grounds, to 1737-9; it is found among Handel's sketches at Buckingham Palace. The other, discovered in the library of the Sacred Harmonic Society in 1857,* and now lodged in the Royal College of Music, London, is apparently a later English copy; it is complete, except for some omissions of detail, and bears the heading 'Magnificat Del R^d Sig^r Erba.'

Handel's MS., it is now generally admitted, was not the original; it was a copy made from some earlier music.† There are some omissions in the R.C.M. copy, which have suggested the idea that this was made, not from a score, but from the separate parts. Chrysander, indeed, maintained that Handel also copied from parts, nay more from printed parts. Clearly these contentions are of no vital importance, for Handel would be at least as likely to have the parts of his own work, as of a work by some Erba, and the printing presses of Italy or England would be open to all, without distinction of nationality. Yet the reasons which Chrysander has given are decidedly curious.

In his edition he reproduced one page of Handel's MS. in facsimile. This page concludes with the symphony at

---

* Previously sold at the sale of Mr. George Gwilt. *Notes and Queries*, March 6th, 1858.

† The consensus of Dr. Chrysander and Mr. Rockstro as to the hand-writing may be taken as fixing (provisionally, at least) the date ; while the incompleteness and other reasons forbid our regarding this MS. as the sole authority.

the end of the 'Deposuit potentes.' But this 4-stave symphony does not quite reach to the end of the last lines. Consequently there would, in the ordinary course, be a vertically oblong empty space formed by the ends of the four bottom staves. Handel, however, had already earmarked this space for the insertion of a fragment for viola, which, if put in in the usual way, would have required an extra stave, with the result that the movement would have had to trespass on the next page. Economy inciting him, therefore, he has written this viola part on the ends of the lines in succession, and has, of course, prefixed the rests, 21 bars long, to indicate the place of entry of this fragment in the score. It seems to be on account of this viola part that Chrysander has photographed the page—at least I can discover nothing else that could possibly have any relevance—and from a passage in his biography (iii, 88) one suspects that he vaguely connected this purely accidental vertical arrangement with the vertical arrangement found in old part-books. Yet vague the idea must have been. For what possible motive could Handel have had, in any case, for reproducing this arrangement just in one place? And as for the rests, if Handel had been copying from a part, there should have been 24 not 21; which proves that Handel, here at least, was *not* copying directly from a part. It is a mere matter of counting.* Whether the second copyist used parts will be considered later, but in Handel's case the suggestion seems quite unnecessary.

The stress that is laid on the fact of Handel's MS. being only a copy means, or should mean, that he only made the acquaintance of the work about 1737; otherwise he was

* It was a natural conjecture that there was on the score some indication of the point from which the rests were to be reckoned; and having been enabled, by the kindness of Sir Walter Parratt, to consult the MS., I find that Handel has marked the point very clearly by the words "Viola entre," placed over the voice-part at bar 14. Reckoning after bar 14 the rests correspond exactly. As to the other page which Chrysander photographed, this proves that the MS. was incomplete, but nothing more, so far as I can observe.

surely at least as likely to make a *fresh* copy of a work of
his own, as of a work by Erba. Our first task then is to
show that he had been acquainted with the work for thirty
years, unless indeed he wrote it himself in England or
Hanover.

II.

Merely noting that the rather uncommon final cadence
of the voice-parts of the ' Erba ' duet, ' Et exultavit '—the
second number of the Magnificat—is found in the A minor
Hanover duet, *A mirarvi* (a duet not utterly unlike the
' Erba '), and also in the duet or trio ' Dolce amico ' (*Aci*
1708) let us direct our attention rather to the opening voice-
phrase : —

Now in *Il Trionfo* (1707 ?) there is a song ' Un pensiero '
which has a quite distinct second section, derived so far as
concerns the accompaniment from *Almira* :—

Here then is a resemblance which *might* very well be
accidental, though both examples express practically the
same idea, the upspringing of a cheerful thought in the
mind. But it gives us a commencement. *Il Trionfo* was
perhaps Handel's most important Roman work; its ideas
he would not use at Rome without being aware of the fact.
We may examine therefore the second number of the cantata, *O! come chiare e belle* (Ap.—May, 1708). [This
cantata Chrysander seems to have regarded as a pastoral;
it is really a political cantata written to urge on the Romans
the support of the Pope in his quarrel with the emperor,
when he opened the treasures of the Castle of St. Angelo,
and reviewed his troops in person. The Romans are
bidden to trust him 'who holds the keys of heaven';
immediately following which is a song, 'Astro clemente'
(O, clement star), the name of the Pope being Clement XI.]

Observe that the instrumental accompaniment is quite
different; it provides a further illustration of Handel's
habit of placing the same theme in most widely dissimilar
settings. We have thus gained a *possible* connexion
between the cantata and the *Magnificat*. What, in conjunction with this resemblance, leaves no doubt whatever,
is the comparison of the symphony of the song 'Tornami

a vagheggiar' in the cantata with the ritornello (the only
surviving instrumental portion) of the *Gloria Patri* in the
'Erba' :—

Let it be observed that apart from the opening theme, we have very similar developments, but with the two features reversed; *i.e.*, the scale passages from subdominant to dominant, and the passages in thirds which start with the same four notes, but then diverge. It is perfectly true that such passages *might* occur anywhere; but it is also true—and this is the really important point in such matters —that they do not occur anywhere; that is, you might search long in corresponding places, after an opening theme, before finding anything as like the 'Erba' continuation as this cantata continuation. However, no one will feel inclined to make the search when it is pointed out that this cantata song happens to be sung by a character called 'Gloria.' There can be no question, therefore, of accident; if the 'Erba' was already written, Handel had acquired his copy before Ap.—May, 1708.

The probable date of *Il Trionfo* (1707), as well as a comparison with the 'Gloria Patri' of the *Laudate Pueri* (July, 1707) might perhaps push back this acquisition still further. But I hasten rather to mention a most singular experience that befell me. After I had written the first draft of a paper which comprised the displaying of the connexion between the 'Erba' and the 1708 cantata, Mr. Sedley Taylor's book appeared, exhibiting at p. 168 a borrowing in Handel's *Laudate Pueri* from 'Tento di spargere' in Keiser's *Octavia* (1705). The resemblance indeed is of the slightest description, and if not accidental, illustrates once more the thesis, that the borrowed material often became transformed almost beyond recognition. Most slight, however, though the resemblance of Keiser to Handel be in this instance, the first three bars of the symphony of this song of Keiser's are *identical* (bass as well) with the first three bars of the cantata extract given above. The key is different and we have $\frac{3}{8}$ instead of $\frac{3}{4}$ time; but otherwise the reproduction is note for note. In the fourth bars the first notes are, of course, the same too, except that Keiser has added an appoggiatura and trill. So that in spite of the proved connexion between the cantata symphony and the 'Erba,' the symphony was really taken from a song in Keiser's *Octavia*.

How can this be explained? The natural explanation is, of course, that Handel wrote the 'Erba.' Yet two other explanations are *possible* (1) That this obscure *Magnificat* had somehow found its way to Keiser, as well as Handel at Hamburg, and that in spite of this double use, and of Handel's carrying a copy with him through all his wanderings, Dionigi Erba still remained obscure. Will any one embrace this theory? (2) That with *Octavia* in his trunk Handel, on reaching Italy, somehow somewhere picked up this *Magnificat* with its resemblance to *Octavia*, which he noted, just as in the case of the 'Stradella.' He was a Glückskind, the favourite of fortune. Now if we were only concerned with the 'Erba' and a composition of Dionigi Erba's could be shown likely to fall into Handel's hands at Rome (or at Florence, if he went there first), this theory might possibly pass muster, if necessary. But it is straining too far our credulity to ask us to accept *two* such pieces of luck. One work at least ought to be abandoned, and Handel's authorship recognised. Only what now will become of pronouncements about style?

At the same time, why a work of a Milanese musician should have found its way to Rome or Florence and have been taken to Handel's heart is by no means clear. Was it that Dionigi was a brother of Benedetto Erba, and that Benedetto introduced the work to Handel? That might explain it, but it would explain it by supposing circumstances which made the explanation itself unnecessary. If Benedetto Erba was thus intimately acquainted with Handel, he would be very likely to invite him to stay at his house, and the simple explanation suggested p. 114 becomes by far the best solution. Let us see what can be learnt about Dionigi and Benedetto Erba.

III.

About 1690 there lived at Milan a Don Dionigi Erba, who in 1692 seems to be described as a *maestro di cappella* at the church of San Francesco,* specimens of his work appearing in Vigoni's *Sacre Armonie* in 1692 (Grove). In 1694 and 1695 he collaborated in a couple of operas. On what authority (unless it be Chrysander's *conjecture*) 'Grove' states that he was of noble birth and an elder brother of Benedetto Erba, I do not know. Quadrio's use of the word 'Don' makes it pretty certain that by 'Don

---

* Presumably the old church which was converted into a barrack by Napoleon.

Dionigi Erba' he meant to indicate clerical character, not noble birth.

Now what do we really learn from Quadrio about Erba? Quadrio has compiled a list of about 170 opera-writers (almost all Italians), yet of these 170 Erba is not one; he is only mentioned incidentally. And we may conjecture that he owes his insertion at all merely to local feeling. Quadrio was born in 1695 at Ponte in the Valtellina (north of Milan); he published the greater part of his work (1739–59) at Milan, and died at Milan, 1756. He has pleased himself by inserting full accounts of some local productions, including *Arione,* 1694, and *Antemio,* 1695. Let us quote his account of *Arione* :—

> ' Molti furono quelli, che a metter in Musica l' *Arione* recitato in Milano nel 1694, per lo compimento degli Anni di Leopoldo I, fecero prova del lor valore. E i Recitativi degli Atti, Primo, e Terzo, furono posti in Musica da *Carlo Valtellina;** quelli del secondo Atto furono posti in Musica da Don *Dionigi Erba.* Le Ariette poi furono messe in Musica, quali da uno, e quali da un altro de' più valenti Maestri di Musica, che fiorissero allora, che furono oltre ai detti due *Valtellina* ed *Erba, Carlo Ambrogio Lonati, Giovanni Ferrari,* il Canonico *Ciapetta,* il *Castelli,* il *Landriani,* il *Polarolo,* il *Brevi,* lo *Scaccabarozzo,* il *Salimbeni,* lo *Scarlati,* [*sic*], il *Gariboldi,* il *Mazza,* l' *Orto,* il *Vianova,* il *Griffino,* il *Bramantino,* il *Gilardino,* il *Ballarotti,* il *Ghielmino,* il *Manza,* il *Legnani,* il *Boschi,* il *Barbieri,* il *Torelli,* il *Bigatti* e il *Mantelli.*'

It will be observed that Valtellina was presumably a compatriot of Quadrio; and that the honour of being among the most distinguished masters fell to a very large army, the only name at all well-known being Scarlatti, if it really is Alessandro who is meant. Let us read the next passage :—

---

* The names here italicised have capital letters in the original.

' L' *Antemio* della Bella Villa recitato in Novara nel 1695, fu posto in Musica da Diversi: e *Alessandro Besozzi* pose in Musica l' Atto Primo: il soprallodato *Dionigi Erba* pose in Musica l' Atto Secondo: e *Giacomo Battistini,* maestro di cappella della cattedrale di Novara, mise in Musica l' Atto Terzo.'

Here again Erba collaborates on equal terms with two other undistinguished musicians. We find nothing to indicate peculiar prominence.* As Chrysander remarks, he was not elected to the 'Arcadian' Academy (founded 1690). Of course he may have died early. Yet Prince Livio Odescalchi, cousin of Benedetto Erba was one of the very earliest members, and Dionigi was certainly living when this prince was elected.

The notice in Laborde, *Essai sur la Musique,* 1780, tells us nothing new, and seems to rely on Quadrio. Gerber's *Lexicon* avowedly translates Laborde, and in this connexion there is a point worth noting. Gerber, it is stated, availed himself of the material which Walther had collected for a projected second edition of his *Lexicon,* of which the first (and only) edition was published 1732. Now Walther in a letter dated January, 1734,† happens to remark that among the very few kind communications sent by correspondents was one from a priest at Como, who gave further details about local Milanese composers. Yet Gerber, coming after Walther, has nothing fresh to tell us about Erba. This is an argument from silence, and must not be pressed. Still the circumstance fits in with the conclusion probable on other grounds, that Erba had no particular reputation, even in Milan, a town not rich just then in musical celebrities.

Benedetto Erba was the son, or more probably grandson

* I take ' soprallodato ' to mean ' above-mentioned '; and even if ' lodato ' were taken to mean ' praised,' it is still obvious that the praise was not excessive.

† Herr Seiffert, "S.I.M.G.," ix, 156.

of Lucrezia Odescalchi, sister of Pope Innocent XI., the Pope of Browning's *The Ring and the Book*. His cousin Prince Livio Odescalchi, Duke of Bracciano, &c., &c., was a very great personage at Rome; he was one of the earliest 'Arcadians,' and in 1693 the meetings were held in gardens lent by him. Being childless Prince Livio adopted Balthasar Erba (brother of Benedetto) as his heir, on condition of his changing his name and residing at Rome [both families sprang from Como]. Benedetto himself took the name of Odescalchi about 1712. What else can be learnt about Benedetto? I shall give first the account in Crescimbeni, adding some dates in brackets:—

> 'Timalbo Stilangiano. Monsignor Benedetto Erba Milanese, Referendario d' ambe le segnature. Poi Arcivescovo di Tessalonica, e Nunzio in Pollonia [1711]. Ora Cardinale [1713] e Arcivescovo di Milano [1712] col cognome Odescalchi; e Arcade Acclamato.'*

After examination of the explanations prefixed by Crescimbeni to his list, we discover that Benedetto Erba was elected an 'Arcadian' at Rome—*i.e.*, a member of the body with which Handel was closely connected during his Roman stay—when he filled the office of Referendario at the Papal court, and that he received the usual further honour of 'Acclamation' on his election to the cardinalate.† Benedetto did not quit Italy till 1711; the Archbishopric of Thessalonica was purely honorary, and was bestowed while he was in Poland.‡ The date of his birth is given at 1670 (or 1679 according to Abbé). We learn from Abbé that he was also cameriere d'Onore at the Papal court, and prior to 1711, vice-legate first at Ferrara, and afterwards at Bologna.

---

* Crescimbeni, *Istoria della volgar Poesia*, vi, p. 414.

† This is not brought out clearly by Chrysander (i, 174). His statement (i, 210) that *all* the Cardinals were 'Arcadians' is by no means borne out by an examination of the list.

‡ Abbé, *Dictionnaire des Cardinaux*, s.v., Erba.

I have not been able to learn the dates of these last appointments, but in the ordinary course of things Erba must have been elected an 'Arcadian' before or during Handel's stay at Rome, 1707-8, and probably in 1709 he was mostly at Ferrara or Bologna. Now in the little war between the Pope and the Emperor, terminated January 15, 1709, Ferrara and Bologna had suffered heavily, and the distress had been aggravated by previous floods and pestilence. When the war was over, the pope had to send corn to those towns. Suppose then that Handel, who was very likely acquainted with Erba, and certainly, we may say, with Prince Livio Odescalchi, wrote a *Magnificat* at the close of the little war in February or March, 1709, it might well have been written at the house of or in some connexion with Benedetto Erba at Ferrara or Bologna.

IV.

I have suggested this explanation 'at the house of' on p. 114. Apart from the parallel 'dal Marchese Ruspoli,' we find 'da' with this meaning in the text of *Agrippina;* and a particularly interesting example is found in a title quoted by Burney (iv., 99) "Fede di Zancla. *Oratorio* nella sollennità della Festa della sacra Lettera, scritta dalla Gloriosa Vergine Maria a' Messinesi." No composer's name is given; and, but for the absolute impossibility, it would be difficult for an ordinary Englishman to resist the translation : 'scritta dalla'='written by.'

The reproduction of the note on *La Resurrezione* by Dr. Chrysander, who is followed by Mr. Rockstro, is not quite exact. Handel, for instance, has written 'Marchese' not 'Marche,' 'Pasqual (e ?)' not 'Pasque,' 'di' not 'd'.' Though both biographers generally quote the signature, they omit it here. Handel, of course, often omitted the signature, or signed with initials. Here, however, there is a full signature in the right-hand bottom corner; but it has an unusual form. It is preceded by the words 'Per il

Sgr.' So that here the 'dal' applies to the Marquis, and the 'per' to Handel. Now on the cantata *Ah! crudel,* preserved in a late transcript, we find : 'Composta a Roma per il Sgr. Marchese Ruspoli da G. F. Handel.' Here 'per' means 'for' and 'da' means 'by,' and on this analogy the 'Resurrezione' note might be made to mean that the work was written 'by' the Marquis 'for' Handel. And a similar note might be read as meaning 'written by Erba for Handel.' However, as observed, there might have been no signature, or it might have become illegible, or been torn off.

Apart from all other considerations I should propose this as a better explanation of the MS. problem than the 'Dionigi Erba' solution. To free the point from alien intrusions, let us put it rather differently. A manuscript has been found in Germany about 1857, bearing the heading 'Magnificat Del Rd Sigr Besozzi'; nothing else is known except that J. S. Bach had once possessed the MS. from which our MS. had been copied. [There is no question of borrowing.] Now Bach, as our tale has it, was in Italy, 1707-9, and was there entertained by many distinguished people. From Italy he brought away no copy of a church composition of any size so far as is known, barring one extremely doubtful or rather exploded instance. On the other hand he wrote an oratorio with a note on the last page '. . . dal Marchese Maffei . . .' very near the time at which he might naturally have written such a *Magnificat,* if he wrote one at all. This note is the only surviving indication of how he might date a sacred composition in Italy after the first four months of his stay; and the similar dates on nearly all his larger secular works have been lost. Suppose lastly that Besozzi [the name of a collaborator with Erba] was a distinguished Italian name. Then, other things being equal, I should think it more likely that the work was written 'at the house of' some Besozzi, than by an obscure composer of that name.

For I at least can only judge of what was likely to
happen by what has happened. It is doubtful whether
Bach brought any such work from Italy; it is certain that
once at least he appended a note which might easily lead
to a blunder. This latter explanation is therefore so far
the more likely. Though the blunder might not always
be made, still it might be made nine times out of ten.
But now comes in a grave difficulty in the way of the
' composer ' explanation. The use of ' Rev. Signor '
in a MS. ascription is, to say the least of it, very
unusual. Why should this be found instead of the
usual ' Don ' or ' Padre '? And why should there
be no Christian name before Besozzi? Christian names
had greater importance in Italy than in England or
Germany. We are to suppose Bach bringing away an
Italian copy from Italy, or else making a copy for himself
from some existing Italian copy. Why, then, should these
very unusual features have shown themselves in just this
of all cases? Or if Bach's MS. had a heading of the
usual type, including the Christian name of the composer,
what motive could a copyist have for making alterations
or omissions? Slight alterations, $e.g.$, R^d for R^o or R^{do}
he might make, but why omit a $molto$ before ' Rev. Sig.,'
or a ' D.' or ' Don ' after it? And above all why omit
' Alessandro ' before ' Besozzi '? Besozzi was not world-
famous like Handel or Scarlatti. On the other hand, if
Bach were merely jotting down a note of place, an uncere-
monious ' R^d Sig^r Besozzi ' might be enough; he would
not be copying anything, and would not trouble about
forms; he might often have addressed his host according
to the customary form ' Rev. Signore.' But ' Rev.
Signor ' in titles is uncommon, even when correct.*

* Handel's original may have had Mgr. instead of the Sig^r, which might
be read Sgr, on the R.C.M. copy. The latter is so indistinct that Dr.
Gauntlett thought he could almost detect a contraction of 'Dionigi' in the
word.

Such questions are not always viewed from the right standpoint. The meaning of the copyist has only a value as assisting us to the original meaning. A certain writer on architecture told his readers of the ' centralone,' apparently some kind of Italian tower. Now there was no manner of doubt about his meaning. Yet some ' ill-conditioned Blotton,' reading one of the authorities from whom our writer had quoted, came upon a passage in which a phrase ' the central one ' had been misprinted ' the centralone.' And he delivered his opinion that there and there only did such things as ' centralones ' exist. And he seems to have been right. But observe that if it had turned out that there were such things as ' centralones,' of which at the same time it was very unlikely that the writer should have heard, the ' blunder ' explanation would still be the more probable.

V.

About style little can be added to what was remarked on p. 156, except this : that in view of the connexion of the *Magnificat* with the cantata *O ! come chiare*, it must at least be admitted that Handel studied the work in Italy, and used its themes. But if so, why should he not have written himself in that style? And if he introduced bad and un-Handelian work into *Israel* in his riper years, why, why could he not have done something similar in his salad days? Dr. Walker (*History of Music in England*, p. 207) has objected to the short chorus ' He is my God ' in *Israel*, but without giving particulars. At any rate Handel has made a certain number of alterations as compared with the *Magnificat* version, so that at least for him the resultant chorus was good enough.

How Chrysander heartened himself to pronounce that the work was written before the close of the seventeenth century, I do not understand. If Dionigi Erba himself lived till 1710 he might have written then just as he wrote in 1690. And had Chrysander considered the use of the oboes? Had he noticed these often, or ever, in Italian church music before 1700? This point it is not worth while to labour, for Erba may have lived till 1710 or till 1750, for all apparently that anyone knows. Chrysander's argument for a connexion with Milan, because the work is written for a double choir, would break down in any case through the discovery of the double-choir chorus at the end of the *Nisi Dominus* (1707). But the use of two organs was not confined to Milan. Burney mentions two organ-lofts at Padua, and seems to speak of six at St. Mark's, Venice.*

But the use of the oboes raises the further question : did they exist at all in the earliest version of the *Magnificat,* or were they added by Handel about 1738? In the R. C. M. copy the top line, marked for oboe, is, for some reason, vacant throughout the work; this has been the principal reason for supposing the copyist copied from parts, the oboe parts and one or two other fragments being lost. Still this would be accounted for, if Handel added oboes in a revision about 1738, and merely indicated the fact on the old score, without writing there the new parts. We need not absolutely reject the ' parts ' theory; there would be no reason in any case, why fragments of the original score should not have survived as well; and yet objections present themselves. For one thing, how without a score, did the copyist discover that there ever were any oboe parts at all? Then there is this difficulty. The two violin parts are written on the same stave, though they occasionally cross. This is natural enough if there was a score, but scarcely natural, if there were only separate parts to copy from. Are we to suppose that paper with more than twelve staves was unprocurable? Handel also

---

* *Tour in France and Italy*, pp. 143, 181. And from Mr. Sedley Taylor's book, p. 91, it would appear that Mr. E. J. Dent has frequently observed this arrangement.

adopted the same arrangement in the first three numbers, and placed the oboes below the viola. Afterwards, in the choruses, he placed Oboe I. and Violin I. in unison on the first stave, and Oboe II. and Violin II. in unison on the second. The position of the oboe at first, below the viola, is worth noting.

Attention may be directed to the ' Tenore uniss.' in the ' Gloria Patri ' ritornello (p. 175). These are written in the tenor clef and the music descends to A, below the range of the ordinary viola. We must, therefore, be dealing with such violettas or tenores as are found in the ' Urio ' *Te Deum,* where the music also goes as low as A. These violettas, the use of which seems to have lasted as late as Burney's time, would scarcely have been reserved, one would have thought, just for this ten bars' ritornello; besides, the term ' uniss.' suggests that they had previously been divided; yet there is no other trace of them in either score. Is it possible that Handel cancelled these parts on revision in his later copy, and substituted oboes? This particular number, the ' Gloria Patri,' is just that which he would have had no occasion to revise: the previous number was copied, though not completely, while the final number, ' Sicut erat,' though not copied, was nevertheless transferred with little alteration to *Israel.* However, there may be no chance of deciding such things with certainty.

VI.

The discussion has resulted in the conclusion that Handel wrote the ' Urio ' *Te Deum,* and that his authorship of the other two compositions is attested by evidence of almost immeasurably greater weight than such as can be advanced on the opposite side. And let him, who wishes to realise this fully, take his seat with pen in hand, and try to draw up a sketch of the history and experiences of these MSS. (if written by Italians) in the light of the facts now brought forward. And let him have a care that the hinder part of his tale does not contradict the fore— a ' malady most incident to ' theories, especially such as have not adventured themselves on paper. Let him not forget to decide whether Handel brought away from Italy roomy chests filled with Italian compositions, and, if so, what was their fate, and why the historians tell us nothing about them; or if the view be preferred that very few were removed, let it be told why the works of Erba and Urio were included in the selection. Let the tale not forget the use of themes from these works in Italy; let it relate whether this was done openly; whether Handel discoursed with Italian musicians and patrons about these treasures; whether his friends knew that he was making this curious selection; and why, in spite of all, Erba and Urio remained as obscure as ever. And when the best, the least objectionable accounts have been constructed, one and one only for each work, then let it be judged whether such narrations, or the alternatives proposed in the present book, do the less violence to facts, and to the abiding laws of scholarship and probability.

APPENDIX.

BACH'S INDEBTEDNESS TO HANDEL'S ALMIRA.*

IT was pointed out in THE MUSICAL TIMES of July, 1906, that Bach must have been well acquainted with the early 1704 *Passion*, generally attributed to Handel. It may easily be shown that Handel's opera *Almira* (1705) was also very well known to Bach, as might indeed have been anticipated, for in Germany *Almira* seems to have been the *Dream of Gerontius* of the opening decade of the 18th century. Except when both draw from traditional sources, thematic resemblances between Handel and Bach seem to be extremely rare, so that resemblances to *Almira,* not distributed sporadically over Bach's works, but confined to a few only, and occurring in clusters, cannot possibly be the result of accident.

A cluster found in the cantata *Wachet, betet* (*circa* 1716) will be first examined. Of this cantata, according to Spitta, Bach seems to have formed a high estimate, as he revived it several times in later years. In the opening chorus (C major) he seems to have taken an unusual view of his text, ' Watch and pray.' It is set as though it were a reveille. Here is the opening of the voice-parts in the chorus, where are found the main features of the movement, the semi-quavers in the second and third bars representing instruments : —

----

* Reprinted, by kind permission of Messrs. Novello and Co., from an article in the ' Musical Times,' May 1907. The alterations are very slight.

wa - - - chet, wa-chet, wa - chet

And here are parts of the opening symphony of the *Almira* air (C major, p. 64*), 'Ob dein Mund wie Pluton's Rachen,' bars 2-4 :—

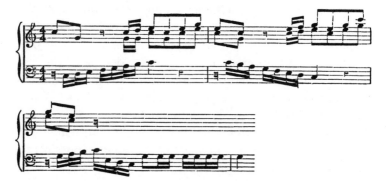

It will be observed that the resemblances here, though palpable, are only such as must occur by chance from time to time. But an entirely different complexion is put upon the matter by the discovery that the second section of the same chorus has also a resemblance to the immediately preceding air in *Almira*, 'Svenerò, svenerò' (p. 63). In the example from Handel's air the opening theme of the first bar has been joined to the essential continuation in the second, to save space, and for the same reason the quotation represents Bach's repetition at the second bar.

* The pagination references in *Almira* indicate the German Handel Society's edition.

Reference to the originals will show that this procedure is quite legitimate :—

In Handel's air the last 'division,' one of exceptional violence, runs as follows :—

Now in Bach's immediately succeeding recitative, after a few bars of the ordinary type, a long 'passagio' on the word 'Freude' (Joy) arrests attention. This word is an almost unfailing signal to Bach to be expansive—his 'teeming joys,' like those of King Duncan, 'wanton in fulness'—but this is quite abnormal, the sudden joy of an earthquake, taking this curiously similar form :—

If the resemblances thus far, occurring just *where* they occur, could be accidental, at least Bach's ensuing air ought to have no similarity to anything in *Almira*. Yet this is not the case. The A minor aria of the cantata 'Wenn kommt der Tag' is remarkable, not only for wide upward stretches in the bass, but for the frequent and unusually long-continued concurrence of a 3-4 voice-part with a 9-8 bass. The opening and principal phrase is this, the small notes representing a variation at bar 7 :—

Wenn kommt der Tag

Now in *Almira* there is only one A minor aria (p. 17). This is noticeable, not only for the frequent concurrence, to an extent perhaps unparalleled in Handel, of a 4-4 voice-part with a 12-8 bass. And this is the opening and principal phrase :—

Du irrst dich, mein Licht

The next resemblance would, if standing alone, furnish to many judges a certain proof of interdependence. The six-note theme of Bach's succeeding soprano air (E minor), a theme which is 'echoed,' is much praised by Spitta; he quotes it as it stands in bar 26, where it is exhibited most clearly. Bach constantly introduces slight variations, and I shall therefore add to the quotation from Bach's voice-opening a variation, and the bass continuation in the second bar, derived from the passage from which Spitta selects his quotation :—

Lass der Spöt-ter Zun-gen schmähen, &c.

In *Almira* again occurs, over the same bass, a very similar 'echoed' theme, 'Chi sa, mia speme' (E minor : soprano, p. 45). But as Handel happens to have introduced a modification of the same idea later on as a bass song (C minor, p. 84), I quote by preference from this, as the theme is identical with that of Bach's. This is bar 9,

the repetition of the voice-part after the conventional false
start, DC in the theme, however, being here substituted for
the simple C of bar 9, since they occur in Handel's first
statement of the theme in the voice-part :—

It will be observed that the bass is by no means obvious,
involving as it does the marked collision of the final note
(E or C) with the passing note (F or D).

After a short recitative and chorale we find in Bach's
cantata a tenor air of which this is the opening and principal theme :—

Five pages after 'Gönne nach den Thränen-güssen' is
found in *Almira* a tenor air (p. 89), of which this is the
opening and principal theme :—

In both Handel and Bach the theme occurs frequently in
the instrumental part, and in both it is often followed at
once by a repetition a fifth higher.*

This practically unbroken series removes, then, all
reasonably possible doubt that Bach was acquainted with
Almira, and selected themes from its pages. It will be
unnecessary, therefore, to quote systematically hereafter;
it will be enough to select a few instances.

* Probably the only real difference between the themes is that between
major and minor. Otherwise Handel's might often be *sung* precisely like
Bach's.

Here is an air (C minor) found in *Almira* (p. 40), 'The lips perforce say No, the heart's free impulse Yes' :—

Der Mund spricht zwar ge - zwun - gen : Nein, das Herz frei -

wil - lig Ja, frei - wil - lig Ja, das Herz &c.

In the first air of Bach's *St. John Passion*, the opening words express the same contrast between 'bondage' and 'freedom,' and we find that Bach has chosen the same method of treatment, the 'bondage' being expressed by a bass theme repeated sequentially, while the expression of 'freedom' is given to the voice. The themes, however, are different. But the connection of this *Almira* air with the well-known cantata *Ich hatte viel Bekümmerniss* (My spirit was in heaviness), 1714, is very interesting. In the first two notes of the voice and the succeeding bass we find the theme of the great opening C minor chorus of the cantata; the constant figuring of the bass (2) in the air suggests the repetitions a note higher in the chorus, to introduce which persistently, however, Bach has changed the time from 3-4 to 4-4. At exactly the same quaver Handel's voice-part and Bach's soprano part drop a fifth— (gezwun)-gen Nein (das Herz)—(Bekümmerniss) in mein (em Herzen). The downward sequential continuation is illustrated at Bach's bar 31, &c., the abbreviations being necessitated by the 4-4 instead of 3-4 :—

hat - te viel Be - küm - mer - niss, Be - küm - mer - niss

ich hat - te viel Be - küm - mer - niss, Be - küm - mer - niss

In the second, cheerful section of the chorus we find again Handel's '(frei)willig Ja' reappearing as 'Meine Seele,' and constituting the important feature of Bach's theme :—

dei -ne Tröstungen er -quicken mei-ne See - - - le, meine See- le,

At the first statement, here quoted, Handel's order is reversed, but in the subsequent entries it is restored.

Apparently, however, this was not the first occasion on which Bach had derived a theme from this air. In another cantata, *Uns ist ein Kind geboren*, believed to have been written rather earlier, the first chorus, A minor (after an instrumental concerto), has this theme :—

Uns ist ein Kind ge - bo - ren, ein Sohn ist uns, ein Sohn ist

Nor can there be any doubt here, for after an aria comes a second chorus, 'Ich will den Namen Gottes loben,' which commences like a duet, and is palpably like the duet 'Ich will gar von nichtes wissen' (pp. 37-39), which stands separated only by a short recitative from the above air 'Der Mund spricht zwar.' That the intervening cantata aria 'Dein Geburtstag ist erschienen' was itself suggested by a duet near the end of *Almira*, 'Mein Betrüben muss ver-schwinden' (p. 113), will only be clear when the dialogus or duet in *Ich hatte viel Bekümmerniss*' has been closely compared with this *Almira* duet, with the immediately preceding air 'Ich brenne zwar' (p. 112), and with the number immediately preceding the air, the duet 'Spielet, ihr blitzenden' (p. 110). Bach has commenced with modi-fications of the two opening phrases of the air, Handel's bold opening leaps of a sixth or a fourth being reserved till later on in the dialogus. He has, then, with less than his usual sense of congruity, branched off into a charming phrase derived from the most striking phrase of the duet 'Mein Betrüben,' reserving, however, like Handel, a slight turn which considerably enhances the beauty till the end of the duet. (Handel's close is obviously intended—notice the bass and the violin accompaniment—to be a variation of the earlier phrase.) Bach's middle section, and the tenor air 'Erfreue dich' (Rejoice, O my spirit), which has in part the same words as this middle section, are mainly based on the opening melody for tenor of the duet (p. 110). The close of Bach's tenor air with the words 'verschwinde, du Schmerze,' is rather more pointed than Handel's corresponding phrase, but it is found (in the minor) in the second section of the air 'Der Himmel wird strafen' (p. 73), with the words 'verborgene Tücke.' The voice in this *Almira* air follows on with a very bold and striking, though simple, passage, with the words 'verstören, verkehren, versehren, verheeren.' From this passage the theme of Bach's final chorus, which succeeds the tenor air, with the words 'Lob, und Ehre,' &c. (Praise, and honour, and glory, and power) seems to have been derived; note the 'heavenly length' to which the little iterated figure attains in each movement. Attention may also be drawn to the resemblances between the bass (the chief feature) of the middle section of the tenor air 'Bäche von gesalznen Zähren' (Fast my tears) and the persistent bass of 'Vollkommene Hände' (p. 26); between 'Harre auf Gott' (Hope thou in God) and 'Zürne was hin' (p. 21); between 'dass er meines Angesichtes' (For he is the help of my countenance)—theme and counterpoint—C minor, and 'Chi più mi piace' (p. 11, first two voice-phrases), C minor; and between the chorus 'Sei nun wieder zufrieden' (Now again be thou joyful), G minor, and the G minor chaconne (p. 6).

It was the resemblances between *Almira* and Bach's *St. Matthew Passion,* which first directed my attention to the subject. Leaving out of account recitatives, chorales, and the treatment of chorales we find another practically unbroken series of slight resemblances in the first part of the *Passion*. Compare the arioso ' Trinket Alle daraus ' (Drink ye all of it), and the following air, ' Ich will dir mein Herze schenken ' (Lord, to thee my heart), with the above-mentioned duet ' Ich will gar von nichtes wissen,' especially the ritornello (p. 39); the response of the chorus in ' Ich will bei meinem Jesu wachen ' (I would beside my Lord), C minor, oboe solo, with the response of the oboe in ' Gönne nach den Thränengüssen,' C minor, oboe solo (p. 84); the tied minor sixth in the theme of ' Gerne will ich mich' (Gladly would I be enduring), G minor, with the tied minor sixth at the same point in the theme of ' Move i passi,' also G minor (p. 60), and note the general resemblance of the theme of the ' Thunder and lightning ' chorus to that of ' Der Himmel wird strafen ' (p. 69). In the last case the words in each movement invoke heaven's vengeance on the false traitor ; in each case they consist of five lines of the same metre, the third and fourth lines being respectively ' verstören, verkehren, versehren, verheeren, dein zeitliches Glück ' (*Almira*), and ' zertrümmre, verderbe, verschlinge, zerschelle, Mit plötzlicher Wuth ' (*Passion*).

The *Almira* air is the longest and one of the most important in the opera, so that the resemblance of words could hardly fail to strike Bach, and influence the style of his treatment.

That ' Gönne nach den Thränen-güssen ' was fresh in Bach's recollection might in any case have been suspected, since later on in the *Passion* we find one of these extremely rare ' echoed ' themes with the curiously similar opening words ' Können Thränen meiner Wangen ' (If my tears).

Of greater interest, however, is the comparison of ' Erbarme dich ' (Have mercy, Lord, on me) in the *Passion* with ' Geloso tormento ' (*Almira*, p. 28). Here are the opening bars of the *Almira* air after the introductory symphony. To the oboe part additions have been made, derived from the corresponding places in the symphonies, and this has necessitated the transposition of the last notes by an octave. The second voice-phrase has also been omitted for the sake of clearness :—

As is usual with Bach the melodic skeleton is here so much ornamented with variations from time to time that quotation is made difficult. Bar 39 seems to exhibit it in the simplest form :—

Handel's air is in the *da capo* form, and Bach's may for practical purposes be regarded as such, as the general scheme of the third part is the same as that of the first. The scheme in both arias, after the introduction, is :—
(*a*) A section of four bars ending on the dominant chord.
(*b*) At the beginning of the fifth bar a new phrase, formed on the tonic ninth, quickly reverting, however, to the first section, with slight modifications. Handel compresses this into four bars, but Bach, who repeats the whole of the first section, takes six. In neither aria is this tonic ninth phrase repeated before the repetition in the third part.

(c) A four-bar section, in which the predominant descent of a fourth is treated sequentially. Handel gives this mainly to the voice, Bach to the instrument. Apparently Handel's voice-part at the end of bar 4 of the quotation supplied a hint for this section in Bach. Of course the treatments are enormously different.

Bach's symphony being two bars the shorter, the movements start level again at the second part. Handel's sixth bar is quoted :—

Now at Bach's sixth bar we find also the same rather rare modulation to the supertonic minor,* effected moreover in a manner almost identical. Bach's crotchet leading note, taken by the instrument, fails to rise, and the voice-part hurries down to the bottom, like the shameless stone of Sisyphus :—

That this should have happened by accident is beyond all reasonable probability. Handel adds a few bars more, but Bach proceeds at once to the third part.

A sidelight is thrown on this last example by the cantata 'Liebster Gott' (When will God recall my spirit?), believed to have been written before the Passion. The first air in this cantata, ' Was willst du dich ' (And why art thou, my soul, so fearful ?), has a decided likeness both to the Passion and the Almira airs, though on that ground alone a positive assertion would be hardly justifiable. This air is succeeded, however, after a short recitative, by another aria, ' Doch weichet' (Yet silence). Spitta suggested that

* Rare, that is, in a minor key.

the theme of this was derived from one in an opera by
Lotti, *Alessandro Severo*. But it has an equally strong
likeness to the theme of 'Ich will euch verdammen,' eight
pages farther on in *Almira* (p. 36), and the curious resemblance of opening words removes all doubt as to the real
origin. In *Almira* the 'former flames' are directed to
vanish (weicht); and in the cantata on the 'foolish vain
cares' is enjoined a like disappearance (weichet).   I quote
the themes in each case, the upper notes in Bach's theme
representing the slight variations in the instrumental form :

Ich will euch ver-dam-men, ihr vor - i - gen Flammen, weicht immer, weicht immer da - hin

Doch wei - chet ihr tol - len ver - geb - lich-en Sor - gen

It will be noticed how the semiquavers at the end of Bach's
theme recall Handel's semiquavers; indeed, similar semi-
quavers occur frequently in Bach's accompaniment.

NOTES.

NOTE A.—HARMONY.

Handel was naturally acquainted with the usual knowledge of his time. He resolves his suspensions upwards, downwards, or ornamentally with freedom, not infrequently anticipating in an upper part the upward resolution. He accents passing notes, uses auxiliary notes above or below the harmony note, follows passing notes by a note not part of the chord but an anticipation of the next chord (*e.g.*, *Belshazzar*, 'Ye tutelar Gods,' bar 22). He occasionally writes auxiliary notes in contradiction of the harmony note (e.g., *La Resurrezione*, p. 57, bar 1). As passages illustrating freedom of a kindred nature might be noted *Deborah* 'O the pleasure,' opening bars; and Chaconne in G, Variation 55.

Handel uses the rather rare supertonic, mediant, and submediant 6—4's, and the usual chromatic triads, except perhaps the major triad on the leading-note. The last inversions of the French and German 6ths are found in the early *Passion;* the German also in *Samson*, with enharmonic modulation, 'My genial spirits droop.'

Handel does not often use chromatically modified chords for special effects; but some quotations might be made, for instance, *Cuopre tal volta* (G. H. S., 52, 1, p. 121):—

turbato il rio si duo - le   e il triden-ta-to Di-o vo - ra - gi - ni

&c.

Observe the chromatic alteration, C natural instead of C sharp, to express 'duole' = 'grieves.' Another example is found, G. H. S., 52, 2, p. 122 :—

di   re-go-la al tu-o   co   re   che di don - na   l'a -mo- re

The previous chord is that of G sharp. Chrysander (Preface to this volume of cantatas), thinking something wrong, proposed to cancel the two B sharps, and the A sharp, and to add a natural to the E at the end of the bar. He says the passage may then perhaps be acceptable. But I cannot think the result in any measure justificatory of the extraordinary violence of the method. The G natural in the bass seems to be merely a chromatic modification of a G sharp, the seventh of A sharp.

From a number of passages in which 11ths or 13ths are used, the following may be selected (*Dixit Dominus*, 1st chorus, close of voice parts) :—

NOTE B.—THE LATER PASSION.

From Mainwaring's catalogue this *Passion* is absent, and it seems to be unnoticed by Hawkins and Burney, except that Burney in his Commemoration sketch mentions works in the collections of the Earl of Aylesford and Sir Watkin Williams Wynn, among them being an *Oratorio della Passione*. Yet it must have been esteemed by the royal family, seeing that a copy was specially presented to Haydn by the Queen in 1795.

This omission in the English catalogue, coupled with the fact of the language being German, was perhaps the cause of Chrysander's ascribing it to a supposed visit to Germany, paid by Handel in 1716. But he quotes no evidence for this visit; Mattheson writes of one about 1717, it is true, but the circumstances do not seem to fit in well with the date 1716.

The real data seem to be these:—

(1) Mattheson says it was composed (verfertiget) in England, and sent to Hamburg by post (*Ehrenpforte*, p. 96).

(2) In the same passage he says that in 1718 it had been long at Hamburg.

(3) A Hamburg text-book of 1719 places it in order of time before the setting by Telemann (1716)*

By these data the composition is placed in England, and not later than Easter, 1716; that is, *before* the supposed visit to Germany in the summer of that year. No doubt such statements may be rejected, on sufficient cause being shown; but Chrysander seems to offer no evidence or arguments whatever for regarding the work as written in Germany in the summer of 1716, and merely copied out and sent to Hamburg from England in 1717.

I see no likelihood in Handel's troubling to compose a *Passion* in the summer. And for whom should he compose it? If it be said that the people of Hamburg wrote to beg him to set Brockes' text, they could send rather more easily to England than to a floating address in Germany. However, to accede to such a request, if made, was by no means a common thing with Handel; in fact, there seems to be no recorded instance of his composing a large work which he did not conduct in person. All the circumstances point to the work's having been written in England, for performance in England before the train of Germans, who came over with the king in 1714, most of them, like the king, probably speaking no English.

That English performances there were, we may believe with sufficient confidence for other reasons. Not only were there several manuscript copies in England, but they *differ completely in one chorus* from those found in Germany. It is extremely unlikely that Handel should have made the change, except for purposes of performance. The chorus eliminated was perhaps found too difficult for the singers (who might not have had much

* Chrysander, i, 448-9.

training). At any rate a simpler setting is substituted in the English copies.

Chrysander suggested that the opera *Silla* (also unnamed by historians) may have been privately performed at the Earl of Burlington's house. The peculiarly elaborate staging required creates here a difficulty; but to private performances of works such as this *Passion* it is difficult to conjecture any obstacle. The newspapers would be unlikely to mention them.

NOTE C.—THE CARLO CANTATA.

The existing text is as follows:—

Aria.

(Giunone) Io languisco fra le gioje,
           io mi struggo fra' piacer.
           Che non più crudi lamenti,
           nè più lacrime a torrenti
           spargerà mondo guerrier.

(Giunone) Al diletto, al diletto, ed al giubilo la giù si dia ricetto.

Astrea.   De' gran Numi al comando, fraude, inganno, livor itene in bando.

Mercurio. Rapido impenno i vanni, l' alto decreto a publicar nel suolo.

Minerva. Cinta d' ulivi, anch' io ti seguo a volo.

(Giove). Il Teutonico Marte, la Britanna Bellona, i Batavi penati che, coll' Ibero Alcide, al vacillante ciel porsero il dorso, dian legge al mondo, alla lor gloria il corso; e' l Celtico Titano cogl' Iberi Tifei pieghino la cervice a' detti miei.

Astrea.   E a giorno sì giulivo, porga alloro guerrier baei* all' ulivo.

* So Chrysander's edition ; probably a misprint for 'baci,' which seems to be the reading of the autograph. Otherwise I take Chrysander's version as representing Handel's.

Duet.

{Minerva
{ Giove

Non più barbaro furore con orribile fragore
turbi all' orbe dolce quiete,
ma sparisca il fier rigor.
Sol ulivi trionfanti,
Sol allori festeggianti
sian le mete di grand' alma e nobil cor.

Giunone. Serenatevi, o sfere, tranquillatevi, o mari; e voi
dell'orbe gloriosi campioni, che sott'elmi e loriche,
con gloriose fatiche, sangue e sudor versaste,
festeggiate e ridete, ch'è già scritta nel ciel la
vostra quiete.

Aria.

(Giunone). Col valor d'un braccio forte
Deste al mondo libertà.
Nè soggetta all' aspra morte
vostra gloria mai sarà.

Mercurio. Nell' eterno decreto, più non vedrà vuotarsi dalle
vene i tesor, languido il mondo; per inaffiar col
sangue, in un palme e cipressi; smorzar fiamme
superbe e smaltar di rubin ne' campi l'erbe.

Aria.

Mercurio. Se quì il Ciel ha già prefisso
bella pace, alta pietà,
Secol d'or, fuor del suo abisso,
lieto omai risorgerà.

Giove. Valorosi campioni, se dell' eterea mole, ne' gabinetti
eterni, glorioso risuona il vostro nome, in qual
rimota parte sin' nell' atro profondo per forzarlo
agli applausi giunto non fia, non che per tutto
il mondo.

Aria.

Giove. Un sol angolo del mondo,
che ammirando, festeggiando,
non risuoni il vostro nome,
insegnatemi dov' è.
Se atterraste, debellaste
duci invitti, quell' orgoglio,
che nel soglio fasto sol ascender fè.

Aria.

(Astrea). Echeggiate, festeggiate,
Numi eterni, in questo dì!
Quello che sfidò le stelle,
cor rubelle,
fulminato al fin sparì.

Giunone. Con monili di gloria, intrecciatemi il crine, e voi,
l' occhiuta pompa, alati miei destrier pronti
spiegate, per condurmi a quel soglio, ove a Carlo
l' Augusto, erario di virtute, miniera di valore,
unir voglio in gran copia i miei tesori, far che
l' Indo rubelle baci sommesso le reali piante; e
a piedi di quel trono, in corso vago che'l Gange
ed il Pattol tributi 'l Tago.

Aria.

(Giunone). Con linfe dorate, fra sponde beate,
scorrino al regio piè
Gange e Pattolo.
Dall' acceso al polo algente
che canti ogni gente,
il rege d' Iberia è Carlo solo.

Minerva. Io, ch' il core di Carlo ad alte prove accesi, e de' studi
più eccelsi, colmai quell' alma (onde men chiar
risuona il mio nome nel mondo) qual' onor potrò
dargli? Ah! che volgare onore già non si deve,
a chi volgar vestigi nel sentier della gloria unqua
non stampa; sia dunque dell' eroe l'unica laude,
saper ch'il cielo a suoi trionfi applaude.

Aria.

Minerva.   Anche il ciel divien amante
del valor, della virtù.
Ed un alma ch' è costante
Sa ben giungere quassù.

Astrea.   Vano desir di gloria, s' Astrea non ha per guida, vortici
di rovine apre al suo piede.   Io, ch' all' Austriaca
prole con poppe di pietà nettare porgo, spinsi
Carlo alla gloria ; e su quel trono sarà eterno il
suo vanto che scorta gli fu Astrea . . .

The music ends with two quaver C sharps ' (As)trea,' over a
bass crotchet G, the previous chord being the dominant 7th of
A major.   Some pages at the end are probably missing, as well
as the beginning of the symphony of the first aria.

As the first sheet is numbered 6, Chrysander in his edition
suggested that a large section at the beginning, indeed the
greater part of the cantata, was missing, but according to all
appearance very little can be wanting.   The gods we find have
just descended to announce peace to mortals.   As a result the
Austrians, British, and Dutch are to give laws to the world,
while the Celtico Titano (Louis XIV.), and his party are to bow
their necks.   Carlo is acclaimed as *alone* King of Spain.   The
valiant soldiers, who are now to rest from toil and fighting, occupy
a prominent place.   It is clear that we have to do with some
stage in the war of the Spanish succession (1701—1713).

That the cantata has nothing to do with the peace of Utrecht
is obvious, for by that treaty not the Archduke Charles (Charles
VI.), but *Philip* became sole king of Spain.   Again, it cannot
refer merely to the *proclamation* of Charles as king, whether at
Vienna (1703), or at Barcelona (1705) ; such proclamations had
nothing to do with peace ; besides, Handel was in those years at
Hamburg.   It must have been written after 1706, and indeed
after 1708, for, as Chrysander points out, much of the music is
merely adapted from cantatas written in 1708 or 1709.*   The
date is between 1708 and 1713.

* Two airs are also repeated with little alteration of music in *Il Pastor Fido*,
which seems to fix the cantata as written before November, 1712.

Practical considerations make 1712 and 1711 impossible. In April, 1711, Charles became emperor on the death of his brother Joseph. This caused his chances of becoming king of Spain to approach zero, for the English and Dutch, wishing to keep Spain independent both of France and Austria, had now no object in continuing the war. Moreover the allies had been for some time losing ground against the French; the battle of Villa Viciosa (Dec. 10, 1710) made Philip's position in Spain secure. Charles again is only spoken of as king in the cantata; there is no reference to him as emperor. He is called 'Augusto,' it is true, but had he been emperor we should have expected 'Augustissimo,' or 'sempre augusto.'* Again, Handel in those years was in England or at Hanover, and it is scarcely credible that the Austrians or Italians should have sent him a text to be set to music and returned. And had the Hanoverians or English themselves wished to celebrate peace by performing an Italian cantata—a very unlikely thing—we should find praise of the elector or Queen Anne. It is the soldiers and Charles alone who are celebrated.

And this fact practically forbids us to think of Vienna as the place of performance in 1710 or 1709. A cantata for Vienna would have contained praise of the emperor Joseph. From every point of view we are forced to conclude that the cantata was written in and for Italy, before Handel returned to Germany. That it was not written for Rome, Florence, or Venice is clear; these powers had been neutral or inclining to the French; moreover, in such a case there would have been some reference to them in the text; and further, the Austrian soldiers would only be in Austrian territory, that is, Naples or the Milanese.

As Handel left Italy in 1709 or very early in 1710 we must

---

* The term 'Augusto' seems to have been widely applied, even to electors. Mainwaring speaks of the august house of Hanover. Cf. Letters of Italian musicians, quoted by Herr A. Einstein, 'S.I.M.G.', ix, 417, 421. 'Know, Britons, an Augustus reigns,' writes Young of George II, with no reference to literature. In another cantata of Handel's, *Mentre il tutto*, Fileno, who cannot be supposed an emperor, is addressed as 'o augusto.'

look for an occasion in 1709. This we find in May, 1709, when in the universal opinion an Austrian triumph was assured. If any suggestion be made that Handel was still in Italy at the time of the negotiations of Gertruydenburg (March—July, 1710), the only effect would be to exclude Naples as the place of performance.

But in any case the reasons for preferring Milan to Naples are strong. (*a*) According to the most probable chronology Handel had not stayed more than six months at one place before he reached Naples, May—June, 1708. ' The nature of his design in travelling made it improper for him to stay long in any one place,' says Mainwaring, p. 51, and little as the statement is probably worth in itself, the view is plausible. We should have expected Handel to quit Naples before May, 1709. [If *Agrippina* was written for Venice January, 1709, instead of January, 1708, a possibility which Chrysander in his edition does not absolutely exclude, Handel certainly had quitted Naples.] (*b*) *Aci* was written, June 16, 1708, at the outset of his Neapolitan stay; if his visit was prolonged we should have expected some further important works. Yet beyond three cantatas or serenatas of no great scope nothing further seems assignable to this Neapolitan stay. We hear nothing of any opera. (*c*) This is the more noteworthy because Alessandro Scarlatti, who seems to have quitted Rome later than Handel, produced two new operas at Naples; one on January 28, 1709, and another in May, 1709.* (*d*) I have not found Handel repeating movements almost unchanged *in the same place* in Italy. He would repeat a Florentine movement at Venice, or a Venetian movement at Rome, but not apparently Roman movements at Rome. Now from two of the above-mentioned serenatas possibly assignable to Naples, *Fillide e Aminta* and *Apollo e Dafne*, he transferred movements almost unaltered to our ' Carlo ' cantata. It is unlikely that he would have done this at Naples, especially considering his previous unproductiveness. (*e*) In the cantata the ' valorosi campioni ' are now to cease fighting. But around Naples there had been no

* E. J. Dent, *Alessandro Scarlatti*.

fighting for nearly two years, and what there had been was unimportant. Only a small garrison could have been left there in 1709. Marshal Daun with the bulk of the Austrian army had moved north in 1708, waging a little war with the Pope, and then proceeding through the Milanese to the French frontiers. It is more natural to suppose the cantata prepared for them at Milan, the head-quarters of Austrian power in Italy. (*f*) Handel seems to have left Rome on account of the impending struggle between the Pope and Marshal Daun. But peace was signed January 15, 1709, so that now at least there was nothing to prevent Handel leaving Naples.

And now must be mentioned what some may think an objection to this reasoning. From the paper and handwriting Chrysander judged (G.H.S. 52.1) that the cantata was written in England ' jedenfalls vor dem Jahre 1714.' As to the purport he could only suggest that it might have been written in honour of the Emperor Charles VI. The fact is, Chrysander had a theory that the use of paper, with a watermark containing a fleur-de-lis and the letters L V G, only began with *Rinaldo*, January, 1711. Yet this appears to be no more than theory. I have not heard that the watermark has been shown to be English; and in any case Handel's attachment to the paper testifies to its merits, so that, in an age when paper circulated freely, a meritorious English production might easily find its way to Italy, or to Handel in Hamburg or Saxony, before he set out for Italy. The cantata stands in the sketch-books immediately before the fragments of *Rinaldo*, and the writing seems neater; however, little stress can be laid on these points. The opera *Silla* is written on the same paper, and of this opera there is no trace in England. The elaborate staging which it demanded seems to forbid any idea of a private performance. Again one would have rather expected Handel to take with him the music-paper to be used for his first English work; unless, indeed, he knew he could get in England a paper, of which he had had previous experience.

If anything could reconcile us to the view that Handel wrote such a work in England, it would be the supposition that he had already received the commission and text before leaving Italy, though circumstances, such as those supposed, caused the project to be laid aside for the moment. And in that case we are almost compelled to suppose some place other than Naples the place of performance; Handel would not have sent to Naples a work largely compounded from cantatas written at Naples or Rome.

NOTE D.

The 1704 Passion.

The genuineness of the 1704 *Passion* has been questioned by Mr. E. D. Rendall in an able paper ('Z. I. M. G.,' vi, 143) He points out that no reliance can be placed on the handwriting of the MS., which is now thought not to be Handel's, and to be merely a copy. Mr. Rendall brings out a number of features which he regards as un-Handelian, and contrasts the work in this respect with *Almira*, written at the end of 1704.

We must remember, however, that Mattheson puts forward a claim to have given Handel hints about opera-writing, and that Handel constantly consulted him while writing *Almira*. And the features cannot, I think, be said to be entirely absent from Handel's other early music. Passagios have not entirely disappeared.* As to repetitions, observe the repetition of the beautiful phrase to the word 'somnum' in 'Cum dederit' (*Nisi Dominus*, 1707). Perhaps such things in the *Passion* were due to Zachow's influence. To the flattening on the repetition of 'zum Deckel' ('Du musst den Rock') I have not noticed any exact parallel; it is probably a 'conceit' arising from the words. Mr. Rendall, I fancy, overestimates Handel's independence. He would hardly come before the Hamburg public for the first time with music written in an unfamiliar style. And we cannot reckon on his taste at 18-19 years of age rejecting what satisfied Bach all his life.

Mattheson, it must be confessed, in giving (*Critica Musica*, 1725) a full criticism, from a technical standpoint, of a *Passion*,

* *e.g.*, Cantatas, 52·2., p. 99 (G.H.S.)

which seems to agree throughout with this, does not mention the name of the composer any more than he names Bach when criti- cising one of his cantatas. The work, however, was certainly a Hamburg composition, the text being by Postel (whose name also Mattheson refrains from giving); it was well-known, as I have shown, to Handel, and Mattheson's vague reference to the date —20 or 30 years ago—fits in well with Handel's authorship. Mattheson's object requires as ancient a date as possible. If the *Passion* was written in 1704, it would be 21 years old.

But what is almost conclusive is the reference to the ' world-renowned ' composer—an expression he often applies to Handel —whose ' authority ' has saved this his composition from fair criticism. ' World-renowned ' forbids any vision of some meritorious but obscure composer; at the most it could, apparently, apply to but three musicians at Hamburg about 1700, Handel, Keiser, and Kusser. For many reasons Keiser seems to be ruled out, while Kusser appears impossible, if for no other reason, from having quitted Hamburg in 1695. Everything points to 'the libretto being written after that date.

Mattheson in the *Ehrenpforte*, it is true, does not mention the work in connexion with Handel; but as Chrysander insists, his account is very selective; he chooses by preference such features as reflect a little glory on himself, and he was absent from Hamburg in the early part of 1704. Besides, in a laudatory notice, he might well omit mention of a work which he had severely criticised. And it may be remarked that presumably he does not mention the work in connexion with any composer.

The score, though bearing no name, seems to have been traditionally regarded as Handel's; and though the absence of positive external evidence may justly demand a note of caution, his authorship seems to me almost certain.

NOTE E.

CHRONOLOGY.

I WOULD suggest that instead of trying to follow the account of Mainwaring, whose mistakes in far simpler matters are astounding, or good-naturedly trying to preserve some small fragment, we disregard it entirely. Really, nice sequences and lengths of stay were extremely unlikely to be preserved by oral tradition, and to this alone could Mainwaring appeal. Handel is made to go first to Florence, probably because a year or two previously a Prince of Tuscany * at Hamburg had suggested the visit to Italy. It would seem a natural course to take, and indeed that is practically what Mainwaring says: 'Florence, *as it is natural to suppose,*† was his first destination'; it seems to be no more than conjecture. Yet many things might cause Rome to be first visited; because it was the chief city, or because the time happened to be Easter, or because Handel travelled with people bound for Rome; I find that the elector of Saxony sent an embassy to the Pope somewhere about this time, to reconcile him to the peace of Alt Ranstadt (September 24, 1706).§ Mattheson says Handel embraced the chance of a free journey with some ' von Binitz.' What we really know from Handel's MSS. is that he was at Rome in April and July, 1707; that he was at Rome, March 3 and April, 1708; and that he was at Naples, June 16, and July 12, 1708. For the rest we must rely on indirect indications.

(1) To Chrysander's reasons for thinking Handel did not leave Hamburg till the end of 1706 may be added here, that a doubtful war was raging over the north of Italy, till the battle of Turin (September 7, 1706).

(2) Chrysander's reasons for assigning the earliest Italian cantatas to Florence seem insufficient. Mainwaring distinctly refers the celebrated cantata, ' Lucrezia,' to Rome, and that is just the sort of statement that might carry safely. I doubt whether a Florentine singer would have been inordinately pleased

---

* Who was this prince ? Mainwaring speaks of a prince, *brother* to John Gaston, the Grand Duke. Chrysander seems to follow him (i, 136). Others call the prince, Prince Gaston. The reigning Grand Duke was Cosmo dei Medici; his elder son, who died before his father, was Prince Ferdinand; the second son, Giovanni Gastone, last of the Medici, became Grand Duke in 1723.

† The italics are ours.

§ Abbé, *Dictionnaire des Cardinaux*, s.v. Albani.

at the chance of depicting the peculiar merit of Lucretia. And I cannot see how Mainwaring's writing of 'Tarquin and Lucretia' diminishes the credit which may attach to his statement. Though the cantata is only sung by Lucretia, Tarquin is an essential part of the subject. Mainwaring does not profess to be personally acquainted with the work, and is describing it merely in a popular way.

(3) Did Handel write *Il Trionfo* between the *Dixit Dominus*, April 4 or 11, 1707, and the *Laudate pueri*, July 8, 1707? Almost certainly, I think, for (*a*) the blunders in Italian are, according to Chrysander, very numerous, indicating want of practice. (*b*) The tale of Corelli's inability to play the overture suggests the first Roman stay. The overture is really such as Handel did not write later; if he had been a year or more in Italy, and had already written *Rodrigo* and *Agrippina*, he would have understood better the capabilities of the players. (c) Nothing else of importance can be assigned to the period April 4 or 11, to July 8, 1707. On the other hand, between April 4 or 11 to the end of May, 1708, the alternative epoch, must certainly be assigned the rather important cantata *O! come chiare e belle*, and perhaps also the cantata, *Ah! crudel*, written for the Marchese Ruspoli. (*d*) The general style, as well as the comparison of pieces which have ideas which appear also in *Rodrigo* and *Agrippina* strongly point to the priority of *Il Trionfo*. Compare, for instance, ' Urne voi ' (*Il Trionfo*) with ' Empio fato ' (*Rodrigo*), particularly the opening of the second sections, where the curious bit of unaccompanied quasi-recitative in *Rodrigo* is explained by the corresponding bars in *Il Trionfo*. Compare again 'Un leggiardo' (*Il Trionfo*) with 'Bel piacer' (*Agrippina*); the interchange of time-values in the *Agrippina* version was hardly likely to be cast aside later. Or compare 'Venga il tempo' (*Il Trionfo*) with ' Là ti sfido ' (*Rodrigo*).

(4) We may place *Rodrigo* and *Agrippina* with Chrysander between July, 1707, and January, 1708. If Handel left Venice about the end of the carnival, he would reach Rome in time to write the solo cantata *Lungi dal mio bel Nume*, as the MS. states,

'Roma. Il dì 3 di Marzzo 1708,' utilising in it one of the airs from *Agrippina.* [Chrysander, not knowing of this date, assigns the cantata to Florence, i, 195.] Easter Sunday fell that year on April 8.* Was Schoelcher right after all in reading the date of *La Resurrezione* as April 4 rather than April 11?†

(5) If we suppose Handel leaving Italy for Halle in the summer or early autumn of 1709, and making his way to Hanover before the end of the year—the view that he had received an invitation to go there is rejected by Coxe's Anecdotes—we can allow a stay of about a year before he obtained leave of absence to visit England at the end of 1710. Perhaps the account of his staying at Düsseldorf on the way, and being presented with a service of plate—rather an awkward thing to carry about—really refers to a visit certainly paid to the Elector at Düsseldorf on Handel's return from England.‡

(6) On the strength of a newspaper report (quoted Chrysander, ii, 16) Handel is supposed to have left England for the continent before February 21, 1719 (O. S.). This seems unlikely. He cannot be shown to have done anything till late in the year at Dresden. And it is almost incredible that Mattheson wrote to him from Hamburg, February 21 (N. S.), that Handel was able to answer from London by February 24 (N. S.), and yet that this answer only reached Mattheson at Hamburg, March 14 (N. S.) [see Chrysander, i, 451-3]. The February 24 on Handel's letter must be O. S. = March 7 (N. S.), and mean a date three days after the appearance of the newspaper. Even in those days newspapers sometimes 'dropped into poetry.'

* De Mas Latrie. *Trésor de Chronologie.*
† To all appearance it is 11.
‡ For this visit in June, 1711, see Herr A. Einstein, 'Z.I.M.G.,' viii, p. 227.

CHRONOLOGICAL TABLE.

1685.   G. F. Handel born, February 23.

„   J. S. Bach born, March 31.

1703.   Handel removes from Halle to Hamburg.

1704.   First *Passion* (?) and *Almira*.

1706.   Handel leaves for Italy, end of the year (?).

1707.   *Dixit Dominus*, Rome, April 4 or 11.

„   *Il Trionfo* (?).

„   *Laudate Pueri* and *Nisi Dominus*, July.

„   *Rodrigo* (?), autumn (?).

1708.   *Agrippina* (?), January (?).

„   *La Resurrezione*, April.   *O! come chiare*, April—May.

„   *Aci, Galatea, e Polifemo*, June 16.

1709.   ' Erba ' *Magnificat* (?), February—March (?).

„   ' Urio ' *Te Deum* (?) and *Io languisco*, May (?).

„   Handel reaches Hanover (?), end (?).

1710.   First arrival in England, end.

1712.   Second arrival in England, autumn.

1713.   ' Utrecht ' music.

1720.   *Acis and Galatea* (?).

1733.   Quarrel with Senesino.   Bononcini departs.

1736.   *Alexander's Feast, Wedding Anthem, Atalanta.*

1737.   *Il Trionfo.*   Visit to Aix.

1738.   *Saul.   Israel in Egypt.*

1739.   *Ode on St. Cecilia's Day.*

1741.   *The Messiah.*

1745.   Gluck visits England.

1750.   Death of J. S. Bach, July 28.

1757.   *The Triumph of Time and Truth.*

1759.   Death of G. F. Handel, April 13 or 14.

INDEX.

1   subject   1/05